V

Seiðr as Wyrd Consciousness

by: Yngona Desmond

BookSurge 2005
An amazon.com company

For the Folksoul

Table of Contents

Preface and Acknowledgement

This book has been over 35 years in the making; it needed a lifetime of dedication to occult study while living in two realms of consciousness to complete. Even so, the metaphysical interpretations here are at their minimum, presenting unanswered questions, un-worded ideas, and topics that guide the reader into gray areas, purposefully. A great deal more could have been written but that would leave closed an opportunity for the reader and worker of seiðr to continue the journey.

Because there is no prize worth attaining if it cannot be shared, with heart in hand do I thank my physical and non-physical teachers, guides, and mentors; great souls who entered my life, on schedule, for either short or long periods, bringing with them that which I needed most.

Thank you: Parents, for teaching me Theosophy; Grandparents, for teaching me about Ireland and Wales; Japan, for teaching me of the Pure Land; Rocky Mountains, for teaching me inner silence and being; Patricia Crowther, for teaching me English magical history; Te-ate do-yin, for teaching me to recognize and move the energy body; Israel Regardie, for 'introducing' me to Wilhelm Reich and teaching me about Orgone; Swamini Lalitananda, for teaching me inner ascetics; Professor Thomas, for imparting the 'heart' of world faith and mystic traditions; Master Yang Tseng, for deepening my understanding and work with the energy body; Paramahamsa Satyananda and Swami Janakananda, for teaching me Trika, the Secret Supreme; Patricia and Frank Dorey, for being real Witches and spiritual parents; Germany, for teaching me about the Folksoul; Externstein, for being where I first 'met' Tiw and where my soul's focal point became affixed; Stephen McNallen, for entrusting me; Ireland, for bringing me home; Guardians of Britain and Ireland, for teaching me their craft and sharing valuable insight and rare books; Emory University for letting me teach Philosophy; the Brotherhood of the Sacred Hunt, for allowing me to be who I am; Freya Aswynn, for being the soul-sister she is and supplying some well needed motivation for this book; and for those I have not mentioned here, your words and deeds are irremovable threads in my Wyrd.

Forward - Definition, part one

Technically the word seiðr is defined as: "spell, charm, enchantment, incantation; to work a spell, practice sorcery'. Academically it has been described as a "ceremony", a "form of magic", as one of two "types of sorcery" (the other being galdr), a "particular form of magic especially associated with the god Odin", as a "type of magic in the Northern tradition characterized by the use of an altered state of consciousness, or trance-state"; as "the old Nordic form of shamanism"; and "an art that works on the mind and soul". (1) Additionally, a great deal has been written regarding how harmful it may be, which may be biased on two fronts: first from an Ensi perspective, later from a Christian one. For this verse commentary, seiðr will be used comprehensively for all Northern European magical-spiritual practices (such as spá and galdr, for example) that *engage* transcendent consciousness. Further, this seiðr scholar has coined a term to denote all practitioners of this soulcraft: seiðu. (2)

Forward - Definition, part last

"..for at no time during the heathen period did the old faith attain to such unity in the North as to bequeath to us an unshakable body of truths or a logical whole."
- H.R.E. Davidson, *The Road to Hel*

These words address what is found in the Lore - the mythology of Northern Heathen thought - and so includes seiðr.

Where some contend this practice refers only to immoral and corrupt methods, and others avoid definition at all cost, this seiðr specialist and scholar has discerned a definition that suits the scope of this work.

Seiðr is Wyrd consciousness, or the penetration of profound consciousness - the exploration of transpersonal reality - a science or means 'to know or understand' experiential awakening. Seiðr is often linked to the word 'seethe' and is sometimes mentioned in regards to contacting-raising 'powers' or energies that appear to facilitate soulcrafting (such as spá or galdr). Suggestively, this seething refers to the internal bodily and spiritual processes that result in the 'churning-turning' of the worker's soul, or inner being. This inner 'fermentation' - perhaps connecting alu as a mystical potion - produces a creative wave that enhances all the senses, allowing the 'surging' of such phenomena as clairaudience, clairsentience, clairvoyance, and intuition. Psychic abilities being the

5

physical form of cosmic manifestation, the seiðu then becomes a divine mouth piece, an emissional power of outward Tivaric manifestation, of inward tribal spiritual absorption, and of ritual participation with the divine. In short, they actively attune to the inward expansion of frith to produce measurable results.

The practice of Wyrd consciousness, or the impact of the 'past' upon the 'present', carries a profound responsibility which demands an awareness of the significance of life, of the intricate relationships between individual, sippe, tribe, nature, ancestors, and back again, creating a golden ring of great value. Poetically, seiðus explore vast forests of light and shadow, navigate incredible seas of gods and giants, and delve the profound depths and ageless wisdom that illumines our relationship to Ginnunga-gap.

Two challenges in defining seiðr research and practice as a spirit science are the roles of Christianity and Core Shamanism. The former would label all seiðus "witches" - detrimental and external influences - which are not particular to Northern European thought, where wise women and foster mothers were highly regarded and sought after for their many skills. Regarding the latter, seiðr's primary focus is on sippe and tribe, far removing it from the individualistic and universalizing applications of many new age shamanic practices. Seiðr has an anthropology - a progressive growth pattern - one not clearly outlined in the historical record but a constellation of techniques that have survived through mythology and folklore. Seiðr today is a valid reclamation of the Folksoul, a spirit-culture continuum for the enrichment of all Heathens.

Reference
(1) "Ceremony": Davidson, *The Lost Beliefs of Northern Europe.* "Form of magic": Fee and Leeming, *Gods, Heroes, and Kings - The Battle for Mythic Britain.* "Types of sorcery: Munch, *Norse Mythology - Legends of Gods and Heroes.* ".. with the god Odin": Orchard, *Cassell's Dictionary of Norse Myth & Legend.* "Consciousness, or trance-state: Rune Gild Seið Network, from the internet. "The old Nordic form of shamanism": Høst, from The Scandinavian Center for Shamanic Studies website. And, "An art that works on the mind and soul": Gundarsson, *Spae-Craft, Seiðr, and Shamanism,* internet article.

(2) Seiðu, singular: practitioner of seiðr. Seiðr can be seen in Old Norse speja, "to see; to speak; to sing"; according to Grimm (III:1047) this may also mean "to seethe." Relatedly, Old English spyrian, "to investigate", seems to have evolved into French séance. Exclusively, this word can be

linked to 'shaman'; from Tungus *saman*, Buddhist *shaman*, Tocharian *samana*, Sanskrit *sramanah* and *sramah*.

Introduction - History

Völuspá means *Prophecy of the Volva* and is a dialogue between a völva and Odin. During the course of which is related: the creation of earth from the Seething Void, the measure of time and a period of peace and prosperity for the gods, the coming of three giant "maidens" and the bringing forth of humans from trees, the arrival of the Norns and the coming of Gullveig, the first and Great War, peace, and the exchanging of hostages, the rebuilding of Ensigart and the breaking of oaths. (1) After this, 'what is, of necessity' is related. Namely, the death of Baldr and earth's end - which includes the advance of an army of giants, the death of many gods, and mass destruction by flame - to be followed by an earth reborn and the continued appearance of Nidhogg. (2)

Dated to the early tenth century, prior to 1,064 ACE, Völuspá is narrated in the fornyrðislag or "meter of ancient words". (3 & 4) It is the first text of the *Codex Regius* and comprises sixty-seven strophes for a total of 1,593 to 2,096 words depending on the translation. That there exists a wealth of knowledge and wisdom within these strophes has never been questioned. The völva, during her discourse, provides instructive and enlightening, revealed and salient, sublime and profound soul-stirring spiritual truths, which expound the rare secrets of seiðr, inner reality, Folkfaith, and Urlag.

Of all the texts contained within the *Codex Regius*, Völuspá is perhaps the most inspiring - the most elevating in how it lucidly expounds fundamental concepts of Germanic mysticism - for the would-be seiðu. Read with a keen inner eye, inner senses activated, its lessons present an all-pervading wonderfully woven tapestry of intense enlightenment. Like sipping Kvasir's Mead, divine inspiration will be illumined and the discernment of essential esoterica made clear. For those who are seiðtru, this is a great well, a vast treasure of gold, a solution for all doubts, the acquisition of inner knowledge, the realisation of self-luminosity, penetrative insight, and the attainment of the Otherworlds themselves. That this text still exists, despite Christian influences, surviving even fragmented, is proof perhaps of the grace of Heathen gods.

Introduction - Potentiality

Aside from Völuspá's poetic beauty, exclusively it exists as supernal insight into the practice of seiðr; generally, a practice that taps into the Well of Wyrd to utilize energy from every realm of existence for the purpose of healing, mantic wisdom, communication with the dead, prophecy, and control over events. Seiðus work diligently to harness the Ginnunga-gapic energy of all worlds, to understand and live within the vitality of all that lives, requesting and receiving the assistance of spirit helpers, animatedly connecting with the relatedness of all beings and phenomena, living-expressing life as time travelers or the elucidators of evolution, and daily responding multidimensionally often simultaneously. Additionally they may work with spá, galdr, wort cunning, healing, and vardlokkur, and at all times are wayfarers into the realm of death. They are explorers of both the Over- and Underworlds or the hierarchy of transcendent consciousness, or continual presence. Working as healer, hexer, and souls retriever, they are the dreamers of dreams or transformers of awareness.

Seiðr is rooted in shamanic practices, most likely from the Indo-European folkfaith. Well noted in Germanic lore, the Finno-Ugric tribes accepted their Northern European neighbors as students in their mystic practices; both groups came with an existing spiritual tradition, both were affected by the worldview of the other. Of note, the Finnish word *seita* and the Sámi word *sieide* relate both a human body formed from a tree and a ceremonial fetish object. For this seiðr scholar there is great wisdom to be discerned from this idea and how it may relate to the word 'seiðr' (if at all). (5)

Introduction - Translation

This verse commentary is not an exact translation but an instructive study into seiðr. The particular rendition presented here was created from a cross examination of the primary source texts in three different languages: The *Elder Edda* (Old Norse, English, and German), *Codex Regius* (Old Norse and English), *Hauksbók* (Old Norse and English), and *Gylfaginning* (Old Norse and English), where all used to create this translation. (6) Cooperatively, there will be exclusive interpolations based on actual seiðr experience.

References

(1) Völva or vala, "wand-bearer", a wise sibyl of the Northern European mystic tradition who was known for her staff and gift of prophecy. And: Odin, a god of wisdom and war in the late Germanic, pre-Christian period.

(2) Nidhogg. A dragon that consumes the World Tree's roots.

(3) 1,064 ACE. This text influenced the memorial lay of the Earl of Orkney, penned by Arnorr Jarlaskald.

(4) Fornyrðislag. "Meter of ancient words", is composed both with and without a fixed number of syllables per line; usually 4 syllables per line.

(5) Tree. Germanic lore relates how two trees, Ask and Embla, became the first humans.

(6) *Hauksbók*, circa 1334 ACE, written by Hauk Erlendsson.

~ ~ ~

Vol.28-29: *Alone I sat outside when the aged one arrived, the wise Ensi, and looked me in the eye. I challenged him, "What do you ask me? Why do you try me? I know [and grant] everything Odin; like, where you hid your eye in Mimir's Well. Mimir drinks mead every morning from your pledge. Yet, do you understand?"*

Vol.27: *I know all your secrets Odin. I know where Heimdallr's hearing (ear) is hidden, under the sky-reaching sacred tree. There I see a stream overflowing with muddy waters - from your pledge! Do you understand yet? Do you?*

Vol.30. *Striding to my harrow, he furnished me with rings, so the wise-sayings [the sound advice] could be prophecised from my staff; for my consciousness knows consciousness, the existence of everything.*

Beginning with strophes 28-29, 27, and 30, this verse commentary attempts to order the events for the purpose of both instruction and fluidity of events. To honor the seeress, I will use the name she is identified with in most versions: Heið; further, I will return her voice, allowing her to speak in the first person in that this work is an account of her recollection and prophecy.

Heið: Little is know of her except that her name means "bright one; brightness, clear; fame." Time and again she is recalled as 'wicked', and her name has somehow become synonymous with witches or 'evil women.' Yet, heið is also linked with 'heath, moor', 'heathen/s', 'heathendom', and 'heathenism. The word heiðr combined with either himinn or stjörnur means 'clear sky' and 'bright stars', respectively; and her name is related to 'honor', 'honest', 'honorable', and 'worth.' So how did someone whose name indicates 'cloudless, serene' come to be so reviled? It is commonly conjectured that she started as Gullveig, 'gold-draught; golden drink; gold might', who is thought to be the personification of gold, sometimes considered an aspect of Freyja. If so, why would the Ensi - Odin it seems, in particular - be so adamant about killing her with a spear and burning her? There are two considerations here: first, that she was highly regarded by the Wana, who took such slight at her death that they engaged in the Great War; and second, that she was sent by the Wana to enlighten or illumine the Ensi. Though mentioned only once, in strophe 21 of Völuspá, her legacy is a constant source of conjecture. In agreement with Grimm, this seiðr scholar considers her and

Heið as one in the same; further, seeing no relation between her and Freyja other than both being Wana and seiðus, or mystics.

As light she is a symbol of spirit, her name, 'brightness' is nothing less then luminous intensity. As such, she is the manifestation of morality, of the greater mindsoul. Being 'clear' she is the synthesis of All; Heið then is the creative force, the irradiation of Ginnunga-gap.

The lesson for new seiðus here is death and resurrection, of a rite and the right of purification, or the passage that removes dross. Before the condition of seiðr can be achieved, the former life must be destroyed. When this 'past' is erased then a new name is given - perhaps even the esoteric language is heard, the 'song celestial' - which makes way for the acquisition of higher divine powers, especially within the realm of daily existence. (1) Seiðus, exclusively, like shamans must be left bare and exposed, as a corpse, having all personal and social impressions stripped away, all religious and philosophical ideas burnt, so that a more graphic expression may take place. This suffering must occur not as a self-imposed imagining - which exists only as a deranged badge of honor - but as scars of enlightenment or deep moral sufferings that are seen-sensed by those around them. This is not something self-inflicted, other then by their work-deeds, but something that is done to them by a greater agency.

This condition can only arise from complete dedication after inner purification. Seiðr must be more than a passing interest or lay-research or keen curiosity, it must discern the difference between normal vision and spiritual vision, from daydream and night-dream, from pain and suffering. There exists an exacting formula, found throughout the circumpolar shamans (as opposed to the southern hemisphere shamans), that would have been well known to our Euro-ancestors: serious suffering over many years, perhaps a lifetime; unwavering and proven aid from an 'unknown' or 'unseen' source; a return from death (clinical, or real death); unfailing willingness to use extrasensory 'gifts' for the benefit of others over that of self; and the development of additional paranormal faculties. (2) Diligent seiðus are taught by Wyrd when they become involved in the extension of nature beyond Midworld's existence. True seiðus then, live aware of a dark and invisible world where everyday accepted things do not exist or are turned inside out. Beyond illness, death, and deception, they have arrived at madness, the dark realm of the soul.

Alone I sat outside: This is Heið's account of events, Odin did not summon her but traveled to where she was sitting, which is in contrast to

Baldrs Draumar where he uses seiðr to raise the dead: *"Up rose Odin, old bragger, upon Sleipnir he placed a saddle of wool; riding down from there to Hella's foggy earth. Meeting the loud whelping hound of doom, its breast bloody-chested; for a good length of time it bayed at magic charms sung, yet forward rode Odin, earth's way roaring, rushing, he arrived noisily at Hella's earthen large house. He rode to the front, at the east, which is the highest price! There he called [knew] the knowledge of the prophetess' fair wind - skilled with clever charms, with choice magical ballads - until he was assured of her rising, sitting near him, able to listen to what she says. "What man is this to me unknown, who utters besides me a journeying funeral poem? I have been snowed on and dashed with rain, drenched with dew and long ago was washed as dead." Odin said, "Way-familiar I am, son of War-magic, speak to me of Hella's accused [doomed], so I remember well. For who are the fine and fair benches in the hall raised, all flooded with gold?" The Vala replied, "Here stands the brewed mead of Baldr, to clear him by oath with strong drink, to lie over and above the shield of beyond, to grow beyond. Yes! - the god's power is now within the earth. Compelled, I have been cut from my cover, now must be silent!"* - Baldar's Draumer, strophe 2 - 7

Exclusively, Heið was doing utiseti, "out-sitting", a practice defined as *Utiseti at vekja troll up*, or "to out-sit and wake the dead". (3) Out-sitting could be perform on a burial mound, "to sit on a howe", or a high seat, and was done with the purpose of gaining wisdom. Likewise, some Lawspeakers were said to go "under the cloak" to determine a course of right action, a practice generally done at night while covered with a cloak; often, the one sitting-out would murmer or chant. From *Færeyínga Saga* there is an account of sitting-out that includes: building a fire, creating a square of lattice work, and marking the earth with nine symbols within the weaving of the lattice. The seiðu would then sit on a stool between the lattice and the fire. From this can be learned that utiseti involved: sitting out at night, chanting verses, entering trance, and knowledge of symbols and knot work (lattice). Clearly then, seiðus are mediators between the worlds.

Altered consciousness is a must for beginner seiðus; there can be no true seiðr without this connection to greater existence. By participating in two worlds - the Over- and Underworlds - everything becomes doubled or amplified, including all senses and all thoughts.

Odin sits upon Hlidskjalf overseeing the multiverse. Having deposited an eye (symbol of consciousness) in Mimir's Well, he recieves additional assistance from two ravens ('thought' and 'memory'); ever fasting (his only 'food' being mead, or the 'draught of inspiration') and performing other shamanically similar austerities, his insatiable hunger for knowledge is undeniable. Yet, Odin lacks more than foresight. Being seemingly more motivated by dark impulses or sorcery than Wyrd consciousness - the transcendence of seiðr - he may well represent the contrast of one-sightedness to the full brilliance of inner truth. Or, as the verse interpretation relates: knowledge he has, wisdom he lacks.

I challenged him. From the Lore, this appears to be an experienced seiðr practice, to dare another practitioner, to discern who is the stronger and who is lesser, who sees in two worlds and who is one-sighted. Such battles can take place within any realm: physical, mental, or spiritual - meaning, as human or animal, wave or wind. (4) In particular this would have occurred between sippes or tribes, amongst cultures, such as the Ensi and Wana, for example. Even so, there is a difference between a challenge and a dual, the latter often ending in serious injury or death. Which is why expert seiðus must always stand ready against those who would oppose them by maintaining a level of physical prowess, which is an external manifestation of mental prowess, which is a measure of spiritual prowess.

"What do you ask me? Why do you try me? I know [and grant] everything Odin". It would appear from these comments that Heið has already proven herself against Odin, concluding with a statement that is not questioned in turn: 'I know everything.' If Odin had the same information there would be no need to seek out Heið's vast and undisputed knowledge, for even with the assitance of Hlidskjalf, a pledged eye, and his ravens, Odin's abilities appear to be limited.

..like, where you hid your eye, in Mimir's Well. Mimir drinks mead every morning from your pledge. Yet, do you understand?" Here Heið goes beyond validating her grasp of inner wisdom into taunting Odin with his innermost secrets; questioning even if he understands that which he has received.

Mimir's Well: The wise giant and guardian of the Well of Wisdom, whose head represents divine wisdom. Head taking was a common enough practice among the Celtic and Germanic tribes, who are thought to have appreciated heads as repositories of wisdom. Ymir's head became the heavens or the Overworlds, so in the example of Mimir's head - being taken by the Wana - this may represent an appropriation of the power found therein. Seemingly, the head represents personal and spiritual mægen; in particular Mimir's head represents self-inquiry, self-investigation, and great wisdom. This would qualify him as a symbol of logical and philosophical mind, or an excellent learning tool for fledgling seiðus on the importance of deep (Well) and personal investigation, personal inquiry, and painfully honest personal dialogue. For once acquired, they would be awarded with discernment, divine perception, and Ritatrú.

I know all your secrets Odin. I know where Heimdallr's hearing (ear) is hidden, under the sky-reaching sacred tree. There I see a stream overflowing with muddy waters - from your pledge! Do you understand yet? Do you?" Again the seeress stresses that she knows Odin's most private thoughts and workings. The reference to 'muddy waters' indicates transition and transformation. What she seems to be asking him is: 'I see how your pledge (an eye for wisdom, sight for truth) is producing results, is coming into existence. Do you?' Perhaps this last indicates the necessity of patience, of waiting for an outcome to manifest instead of seeking a different answer, as some do; never satisfied with the response given while never truly seeing what must be done inside to match what occurs outside.

Striding to my harrow, he furnished me with rings, so the wise-sayings [advice] could be prophecised upon my staff; for my consciousness knows consciousness, the existence of everything. Giving gifts to those seiðu you seek answers from is traditional; payment completes a circle of energy exchange. My grandDame is a Welsh 'witch' who for many years set her shoes out on the front porch to indicate she was available for whatever work she could for those who needed it. Over the course of a week there would appear baskets of tomatoes or apples, pecan pies or pound cakes, cartons of cigarettes and bottles of liquor (she neither drank or smoked), wads of dollars wound with rubber bands, swatches of cloth, and other items of payment. Each included a written request. She would prepare potions and ointments for gout and rheumatism, colic and diabetes, acne and constipation, along with love spells and birthing charms, and enchantments to insure a better crop, more cattle, or a pay-raise. What she could use for family she did, what she could not became barter for things she needed. A gift demands a gift and the strophe clearly relates that necklaces and rings were given for lore and prophecy.

..upon my staff. Regarding the staff, it is the one unmistakable tool of all völvas, and has a threefold meaning: as a support, a vehicle, and a

weapon. As a support it represents friendship and loyalty, direction and intensity; as a vehicle it represents wisdom and insight within every realm; and as a weapon it represents a cheiftain's war club.

..my consciousness knows consciousness, the existence of everything. Seiður are not at the mercy of consciousness, knowing it as a phenomenon instead of a thing. Simply put, if they do not like a particular consciousness, they change it, for they understand fully how each thought has a result, that nothing is ever lost .. ever, and how similar thoughts create habits or repetitive behavior. Or, at least - they should. Seiður change their consciousness to expand its capacities, to venture beyond self-created barriers, to express new forms and experiences, to weave aspiration and inspiration; knowing fully how all actions are governed by what they know, they seek to discover all they can. For example, trance is an every-moment condition for the seiðr-disciplined-conscious mind - which is truly All-mind - so is well equipped to handle waking-physical activity while it flows through inexhaustible energy. When the student seiðu finds themself alert and responsive on every level of being simultaneously, or living fully in both asleep- and awake-worlds, then a new natural condition has been achieved. This is the optimum state of being.

References
(1) Song celestial. A sacred language that penetrates a shaman's psyche. Reference: *Shamans, Healers, and Medicine Men*; H. Kalweit; 1987; page 143 and 164.

(2) Paranormal faculties. Reference: *Dreamtime and Inner Spaces*; H. Kalweit; 1984; part two: Shamanic Initiation

(3) To out-sit and wake the dead. Reference: *The Codex Regius of Gragas*; the Lawspeaker's Section. *Gragas* is the Icelandic Law Code.

(4) Wave or wind. Similar to shamanic battles. Reference: *Shamans, Healers, and Medicine Men*; H. Kalweit; 1987; pages 195 - 201.

~ ~ ~

Vol.1: *Silence then I asked of the hallowed kindred, and from Heimdallr's children, both high and low born. Agreeable to you War-father, I shall speak of well before the counted time, relating ancient tales, put forth to promote and further all men.*

15

Silence then I asked. Tacitus relates in *Germania,* chapter 11, how this practice is part of early Germanic society: *"Silence is proclaimed by the priests, who have on these occasions the right of keeping order."* By commanding silence Heið is imposing her presence upon the audience - both gods and men - for what we speak and do are not restricted to this world alone.

When achieving seiðr mind - or entering the flow of Wyrd consciousness - the spiritual atmosphere is more than good story telling or performance art, it is primal and sacred drama, which changes the experience of reality. Both a private function and a tribal one, where community is engaged, seiðr engagement invites us to step out of the rigidity of existence, the stress of everyday living, to approach the outer edge of mystery, to touch for just a moment, a small portion of sacredness.

Seiðr work then becomes a combination of divine communion and holy theater in an attempt to weave an environment of health and wholesomeness-holiness; something common folk rarely encounter, or only in brief moments. However, a public session must never be used to create a show, a façade, a situation where the practice is belittled in any way; again, what is done on this world ripples through all others. Beyond all else, seiðr contact creates inner balance and inner purification, so if it becomes abused by pretense-pretend the Tivar may remove the offender's right of passage.

Beyond standard blot or fain, where words may have lost their impact due to repetition, the role of a seiðu is to intensify every sense, to push and stretch and extend energy so that ripples are created and so felt throughout the immediate area, allowing all gathered to temporarily move from normal to supernormal. Artful seiðr draws those gathered into a spiritual atmosphere but not another world. Nor is trance ever a group activity, but one employed for individual access. A seiðr session, for example, is the equivalent of emotional therapy, a revivification and reconnection, therefore best suited in a one-on-one environment, where many intimate elements can be effectively brought together for the purpose of rejuvenation.

..the hallowed kindred, and from Heimdallr's children, both high and low born. This strophe reflects an assembly of Tivar and humans - all wights - for seiðr must be tribal based. Because advanced seiðus are far seeing

they do more then glimpse, but fully explore the interconnectedness of all things. Like a honeycomb, each part connected to the other, life is more than the sum of its visible parts-reality. Mægen resides within every living thing, animate or not, and within these soul-full things there exists a multidimensional aspect. Mægen is life-force, the prime moving force within everything perceived by the senses, both inner and outer, but also independent of the realm of appearance. This is what seiðr does: give the ability to become more aware of mægen, of all consciousness.

There are several outer layers in the approach to seiðr: first is to shift gears, or to change the course of life currently being followed. This is akin to rerouting a river's flow so takes monumental effort, but once done your life can be viewed from an objective vantage. Second there is seeking the definition of dreams, striving to understand the messages you receive, the questions and challenges presented that must be resolved for continuity to continue. Third, this ability must be proven by more then mere psychic ability - which is external and delegated to the realm of Midworld - but convey important messages, verbally, that impact the greater reality. Combined, these layers assist in bringing about reconciliation within you, between the physical-mental identity and the other layers of reality. Some seiðr students touch the outer edge and never progress, never realizing the other Urlag. If there is progression, it is seen in the ability to heal both body and mind - to maintain health at the physical-mental level - followed by the control of dreams, which is directly related to the control of physical reality. Once these initial exercises are mastered, the determined seiðu may be ready to progress further.

Regarding Heimdallr, or Rig, it is wise to call his name when journeying for he guards well the passage to the Overworlds. As Heimdallr he is a "world brightener; home valley", as Rig he is "king" among kings, progenitor of all folk. Born of nine mothers, *Gylfaginning* 27 relates that he "knows well the future"; a novice seiðu would be wise to seek his council. As Rig or Rigr, his energy links the Germanic and Celtic tribes; from *Rigsthula*, or Rig's Thule, his primordial nature can be revealed. In both names, birth is the key component, an outward thrust of creativity that flows with strong patterns of energy, which gushes forth as emotive and intellectual force. It was Óð, Villi, and Ve who animated and gifted Ask and Embla, and it was Rig-Heimdallr who triggered their cellular memory, the structural layers of previous memory experience.
Agreeable to you War-father, I shall speak of well before the counted time, relating ancient tales, put forth to promote and further all men. A request

has been made, a challenge met, gifts received, the stage set - remember, Heið was already sitting-out, so sacred space exists already - the völva is ready to proceed.

~ ~ ~

Völuspá - Before the Beginning

[Interpolation]   *Ginnunga-gap was there, beginning before beginning, seething and churning void of nothingness from which first things merge. Blessed skull and cauldron, radii of zenith and nadir, keeper of three Wells and three roots, soul of all seeds, it is the all of nothing, the nothing of all.*

Ginnunga-gap contains the twin streams of Nifl and Muspel, which are the origins of Hvelgelmir and Urd's Well.   Where they merge, within Ginnunga-gap's center, is Mimir's Well - Grotti's Staff - fount of creative wisdom.   These three Wells and three roots compass origin, outcome, and creative wisdom.

Hvelgelmir is the "churning, whirling shrieker", a vast whirlpool whose rushing creates deafening sound.   Found in Niflheim these cold-lunar waters are both 'past' and subconsciousness origin. Urd's Well is the all-embracing soul that births all souls; hers are the waters of life. Found in Muspelheim these warm-solar waters are both 'future' and conscious outcome.   Mimir's Well waters the seed of World Tree, the teaching-learning tree who's other two roots are nourished by the Wells of Hvelgelmir and Urd.   Found equal distance between the other two, Mimir's Well is a 'third eye', or that which is divine. This Well is the ability to act and understand the act.

~ ~ ~

Vol.3: *First, in ancient time, was old Aurgelmir's fixed abode, [the triple enclosure], when there was no sand or sea, no cooling wave. There was no earth anywhere, no heaven above, only Ginnunga-gap, the seething void, and nowhere herb.*

First, in ancient time, was old Aurgelmir's fixed abode, [the triple enclosure]. 'Ymir' is traditionally used here, however, to fully understand this entity, this verse commentary will return to the older name-form: Aurgelmir.   Ymir, "groaner" is akin to Aurgelmir, "primal-, original-, first-shrieker", which indicates a keynote or primal sound of creation, a sound that birthed light, or that which fertilizes and illumines physical existence, and clearly, this sound births all of Midworld.   Connectedly, this relates to the Indo-European model of sound as the first of all things created, in conjunction with Fire and Ice. (1)

Aurgelmir, exclusively, is the triple enclosure, father to Thrudgelmir, grandfather to Bergelmir. These three are resonance chambers, pure unstruck sound, existing before even the stars were in place. When they merged their sound, a rush-gushing of energy, coagulating within the Great Vacuity, their 'voices' harmonized - churning, floating, and sinking - to form the resounding expressions of terra firma, life, and firmament. In turn, this activity prompted the tonal womb, Audhumla, to manifest. Aurgelmir is the keynote or primal sound of creation, his son Thrudgelmir is the cycle of all life, and his son Bergelmir is the endnote of the world - and so survives Ragnarök as the substance of all renewed forms, the new keynote of creation. Symbolically they are three triangles, one inside the other, which represent energy-wise: bodymind, soul, and spirit. For seiðus, this is a powerful knot working.

Combined, their over-, middle-, and under-tones are the infinitude of all juncture. Similar to the tonal quality of Fire and Ice as they clash within Ginnunga-gap, producing a deafening roar. Aurgelmir, Thrudgelmir, and Bergelmir's collective deafening roar creates a massive echoing vibration that ripples throughout the infinitude of all existence. This cosmic symphony of multitudinal vibrations is the galvanization of all energy weavings.

Linguistically, Ymir descends from 'twin', which would indicate Audhumla, the "primal dusk", as his sister. As a divine pair they would represent life and death, appearance and disappearance, light and dark; and in regards to humanity, mortal and immortal, physical form or that which is perishable, and soul-essence or that which is eternal. Audhumla, a cow, is symbolic of both earth and moon. From Indo-European myth, Brahma, lord of creation, is twined with Vac, the "melodious cow", which mirrors her brother's ability to birth the world from sound. (2) Meaning, the vibrations of primal sound enhances primal dusk to solidify the foundation of all that is made manifest. This is a twofold lesson: first in the importance of galdr; and second, that vocal intonation-chant is best done at sun's setting.

For well-versed seiðus, these twins represent Muspelheim and Niflheim made manifest. Vast plains of churning, boiling, and heaving Fire and Ice are almost beyond comprehension, beyond working with, but to see them as Aurgelmir and Audhumla - primordial earth and moon, the shrieker and the melody - then a clearer understanding of these dynamic forces can be grasped.

Upon Aurgelmir's death, his body being divided to create all Midworld, Audhumla becomes the world's oceans and unseen currents. Being a cow, from her four udders would stream great nourishment, the sublime and radiant light that illumines Ginnunga-gap. Intuitively, the twins - like Fire and Ice before them - are two 'shelves' or planes of existence. Similar to Hlidskjalf, "window shelf", which is the plane from which Odin looks out onto the worlds. (3) Perhaps these three are part of twelve such vantage points, composed of different energy weavings that represent the multiverse.

..when there was no sand or sea, no cooling wave. There was no earth anywhere, no heaven above. Fire and Ice collided into Ginnunga-gap, the resulting sound birthed Aurgelmir and Audhumla, primal force and form, or energy and matter. This verse indicates the order of importance: sand, then sea, then cooling wave, earth then finally heaven.

Sand is the fusing of stellar and terrestrial energy, the vital forces of plant-animal life with cosmic existence; or, the 'meal' produced from the turning-grinding of Grotti's Mill when Aurgelmir's body was placed there to form Midworld. The importance of sand is further seen beneath the sacred posts of Heathen temples where even the soil that supports them is considered holy and so capable of transmitting energy from one location to another.

Sea is both a promise of renewed life and a goal; return to the sea is akin to 'returning to mother', or death. The sea is the manifestation of energy coursing across the planet, mægen that is ceaseless and formless. During dreams the 'sea of consciousness' must be crossed, that vast expanse of unknown reality, not yet molded by mind. Stemming from oceans are rivers - like those that connect Midworld to both Over- and Underworld - great outpourings and inpourings of loss and oblivion, which surmise all probabilities, moving in every conceivable direction. Just so are humans (rivers) the sum total of all their ancestors (oceans) - the individual the sum of all their deeds.

..cooling wave. This denotes calm, serenity, and perhaps purity of purpose. Earth and heaven are dark and light, below and above; they are the quantitative and the continuous.

..only Ginnunga-gap, the seething void, and no where herb. Ginnunga-gap is all things and no thing simultaneously, an unimaginably vast birthing chasm, the abstraction of all abstracts and the supreme principle

of the multiverse. Aristotle referred to the "moved mover"; he referred then to Ginnunga-gap, the central seat of all, an axis with radii, the point of manifestation and emanation. Ginnunga-gap is the pole or mystic center, the unvarying mean that is the cause-eruption of all things. The vast seething cauldron that belches and regurgitates all things, being dipped in which has the ability to return life. (4) This gaping void is best seen through symbols, which are familiar seiðr tools that allow practitioners to access seemingly impenetrable nature.

First, there is the spiral, symbol of evolution; second is the sunwheel, the cyclic motion of life and the succession of generations, of seasons, the tree in motion, and a vast whirlwind. Swastikas (Sanskrit for, "auspicious; well being") are the pole and zenith, its outer 'hooks' acting as propellers that catch then thrust seiðus on their journeys. Third is a triangle, the solidification, even if only temporary, of matter. Combined they create a powerful force of spiritual evolution.

Herb, from Old Icelandic *gras*, meaning, "grass, herbage, herb", carries the meaning of human beings, which further implies value judgments; meaning, herbs are neither 'good' or 'bad' but healing and harming, or medicinal and poisonous. (5) Novice seiðus must understand these concepts by experimentation.

References
(1) Fire and Ice. Reference: *Symbology of Sound*; A. Teillard; 1951; pages 57-63, and 121-134.

(2) Melodious cow. Reference: *Rig Veda* 10.71, and *Brihadaranyaka Upanishad*

(3) Planes of existence. Similar to Indo-European *loka.*

(4) Return life. As seen on the Gundestrup Cauldron.

(5) Human beings. Reference: Greek 'neophytes', meaning, among other things, "new herb".

~ ~ ~

Vol.2: *I remember well the household of giants, when they fed me food with nobility. Nine residing worlds I know - nine far-reaching - World Tree to praise and decorate, before the earth was new.*

I remember well the household of giants. Heið does not say she is born of giants but remembers their 'household', as if she were a fosterling or perhaps being provided shelter.   Further, it is not her household, suggesting the Jotuns are not of her lineage.   By prefacing this strophe with the kindness bestowed upon her by Jotuns, she is acknowledging those who have extended a generous and open hand.   Surely then, she is no Jotun, but an energy pattern that has existed before the beginning of all things. This is important for student seiðus to know: that seeking the roots of knowledge reveals - one thread at a time - the greater tapestry of all that is.

Lineage is important: where you come from, what you have learned, who your teachers are-were, for ancestry defines what you know and how you know it on not just a genetic level but deeper still, within the Folksoul. Inner lineage is that which prompts an idea towards manifestation. Thought, for example, is a lineage, just as words are, which is why 'words have power', even though there exist few who understand this to the point of conscious utilization.   As this verse commentary is read, for example, thoughts and images are created and stored, taking them from print to personal imprint, which explains how physical existence is the expression of communication as clearly as if an object was shaped with human hands.

Giants are akin to the gods and from the Lore, often related, so like the Tivar can exhibit a wide array of character traits. More than monsters and trolls they are also friends and lovers, protectors and benefactors; and in every sense of the word 'giant', or far surpassing human stature-nature. As both a seiðr scholar and practitioner their energy was long ago befriended and utilized, learning and gaining from it something both marvelous and terrible.   Being receptive to seiðr language (aside from speechlessness) - a means that quickly penetrates the greater consciousness - such energies are referred to more efficiently as 'gogs' (1 and 2).

..when they fed me food with nobility.   Heið expresses how the giants gave her 'bread' 'before time', that they took her in and were kind to her before the order of sun and moon, before time was *applied*. Time does not speed up or slow down, nor does there exist noon or three o'clock - these are but intensities of experience, energy patterns that can be relived at will. Seiðus cannot feel otherwise and still practice seiðr, for these are limiting constructs that constrict the threads of knowledge and experience.

Seiður do not predict the future - this is both misleading and wrong. In truth, they follow a particular thread, a current that crosses-connects with other threads - an essential line of connectedness between the social and spiritual, the physical and mental, the Overworld and Underworld - that allows them to journey in any-every direction, even at once. Meaning, by tuning-in to vibrations seiður follow probable outcomes - ever mindful that free will exists - which means the vibration is able to redirect its course.

Nine residing worlds I know - nine far-reaching - World Tree to praise and decorate, before the earth was new. The Nine Worlds and their positions are: 'right' and 'left' - Muspelheim and Niflheim, respectively; Overworlds - Wanaheim and Ensigart, now, stand equal at the zenith. Before the Great War they were located at nadir and zenith (respectively). Underworlds - Jotunheim and Hella, now, stand equal at the nadir. Before the Great War they were located left-back and nadir (respectively); and Alfheim and Svartalfheim, now, act as buffers along the Pole line. Before the Great War they were 'back'. Nine Worlds indicate a triplication of the triple or a reflective and vibrational image of the three primal sounds - now manifested as worlds - that exist within being: body, mind, soul. Nine is the number of truth-troth and as seen from the Lore, ever produces-renews itself.

Regarding the *Nine residing worlds,* surely, from this, can be derived that there exists no single 'beginning', nor will there be a singular 'end', these ideas are distortions of time. Apprentice seiður must learn to focus their attention away from physical reality to better realize the existence of other validities. Individual awareness is but a thread within the greater tapestry, one with a multidimensional richness that is intermingled with threads from other tapestries, other realities, on all three realms of existence. Physical reality is quite real and to suggest otherwise is to deny the existence of Ginnunga-gap, for its pulse pervades all force and form. (3)

These Nine Worlds are positioned within the 'roots' and 'branches' of the World Tree, a powerfully symbolic and overwhelmingly beautiful energy weaving that allows access to the multidimensional realms of consciousness. Beyond being an ash or oak, a lime or fig, the tree is proliferation and regeneration, the continuity and consistency of all existence. (4) Being long lived, trees are thought to contain great wisdom, and their continued growth and threat of death (its bark and roots being gnawed upon) represent the continual cycle of life and death. Unlike other world tree models whose roots are often found in the ether or air above, the Northern European tree is deeply rooted in Hel, the place of ancestry or lineage.

More than a universe, the great tree is the 'physical' representation of Ginnunga-gap, the seething void of all potential; and by extension, reflecting the nature of soul, or more specifically, psychic growth. (5 & 6) By way of example, Heið observes these worlds 'perched in the tree', the ship of trance, or a conduit of inner path working. Just so must seiðus sit above Midworld, poised in the center and caught-up in the flow, not impacted by either Over- or Underworld energies, to better follow the threads that course through the very fabric of the tree.

References
(1) Gog. Runic break-down: Gebo - 'ancestral grace and blessing in all things'; and Othila - 'appreciation and recognition of ancestral law and truth; justice for the sake of justice.'

(2) Seiðr language. A means of communication discerned from trance that temporarily suppresses the transmission of internal dialogue into visual and verbal imagery-expression.

(3) Quite real. Heathen thought runs contrary to some Hindu and all Buddhist ideas on this subject.

(4) Ash or oak, a lime or fig. Scandinavian, Celtic, Germanic, and Indo-European, respectively.

(5) Universe. *Grimnismol*, 29-35.

(6) All Potential. Reference: *C.G. Jung, His Myth in Our Time*; M.L. von Franz; 1975; specifically, *imago Dei*.

~ ~ ~

Vol.5: *Sunna, companion to Mani, came from the south; [she] cast her right hand over heaven's rim, not knowing yet in which quarter her homestead should be. Stars were not certain, having no knowledge where they [should] steer and guide, [not knowing] which place their quarter should be. Mani was not certain, what strength his quarter should be.*

Exclusively, strophe five precedes four in the ordering of the cosmos. Sunna, Stars' Course, and Mani would have no 'direction', no mægen, if it weren't for the position of Midworld; their 'homestead' would be uncertain. It can be said that their leadership was already placed in relation to existing positions within the multiverse, but that has no bearing, no point of power, upon Midworld. It would appear then that Sunna, the Stars, and Mani already existed prior to Midworld. According to current scientific thinking the earth, moon, and solar system are all the same age, approximately 4.5 billion years. However, without an orbit, could Sunna, Stars' Course, and Mani have a 'quarter', be 'steered', or have a defined course without the presence of Midworld?

From a seiðr perspective, the sun represents vitality, she is the source of light - physically and psychically - and so the most immediate image of the divine known to humanity. Sun's shine and warmth and ability to renew all wights, including earth itself, act as an opening, or path to within. As 'Sol', she is Midworld's soul, just as she is the outer manifestation of humanities soul. Mani's role is to contribute towards the growth of green life, equally as he guides the tides of all waterways, the Paths of Audhumla. Just as Sunna is the conscious-visible mind, Mani is the subconscious-invisible mind.

Chandra is Mani's name in Sanskrit and means "luminous bliss", he is said to rule emotions. According to the Indo-Europeans, both sun and moon are male, and in this is an example of the uniqueness of Heathenry's perspective. Of note, western astrology focuses on the moon as a secondary factor when calculating a birth-chart, as a key to the inner personality over that of the sun or outer personality. Eastern astrology or jyotish (a Sanskrit word) places the moon first in that its hourly fluctuation-phases are used to determine the course-direction of daily living. This is of interest because our ancestors viewed the night as 'day', or began the calculation of 'day' based on night, which would have obviously included the phasing of the moon; which is a more obvious representation of the passage of time than the sun's appearance.

Combined, Sunna and Mani share the solstice thread of 'right' and 'left', 'south' and 'north', conscious and subconscious, respectively. Specifically, by 'casting her right hand' Sunna is indicating the south, which is the direction of the right hand. (1) Nor are these two alone. Sunna is closely knit to Delling, or dawn - who is 'east' and consciousness - and her son Day. Likewise, Mani's essence is found in Night, a dark and beautiful woman. Day rides in a chariot drawn by the horse Skinfaxi, and the horse Hrimfaxi pulls Night's chariot.

Stars too are nocturnal, or at least what is seen of them, and appear in groups, arranged - much like cloud shapes - into patterns molded by the mind. Some stars have individual meaning - the Pole Star is an example - other stars are known for their clustered arrangement. Therefore, stars represent multiplicity, and their 'dance' across the night sky, changing through the tides (seasonal variations), is a vast passion play that ever rises as the point of origin to sink again into the 'western shore', or death. As symbols of spirit and renewal they act as teachers who educate those who seek their pathway. Exclusively, stars are the physical, biological, and psychological weavings of elements so unified as a whole they cannot be surmised individually. Simply put, appearing in the night sky, the realm of Mani, the subconscious mind, they are welcome hearth fires that beckon seiðus to join them.

Sol and Mani are the children of Mundilfari (*Vafthrudnismal*, 23), a word that could be: 'time, remember; convey, mark', or 'to remember the passage of time.' If so, then this is an injunction for apprentice seiðus, and all folk, to utilize these two, perhaps three aspects (including Stars), in their daily activities.

Grimnismal 39 relates that Sol travels in a chariot drawn by two horses: Arvak and Alsvid. Their names could possible be: Arvak, 'journey + to be awake, wakefulness during the night; vigil + to stray, hover', or, seiðr-wise: 'travel to the place of wakefulness'. And Alsvid, 'beget + turning; free from burning; singed', or, seiðr-wise, 'turn away from fire-burn [sun]', or 'turning inwards'. This is mystic thinking indicating the sun's brilliance as an opening to greater awareness.

Julius Caesar, from *De Bello Gallico* 6.21, relates how the Germanic tribes 'worshipped' fire, sun, and moon: *"The customs of the Germans differ widely from those of the Gauls; for neither have they Druids to preside over religious services, nor do they give much attention to sacrifices. They count in the number of their gods those only whom they can see, and by whose favors they are clearly aided; that is to say, the Sun, Vulcan, and the Moon."* The Roman equivalent of Vulcan is a god of fire and the forge, volcanoes, arms-armor, and iron. He was celebrated during the autumnal equinox in ancient Rome (the Vulcanalia) and there still exists a temple to him in the Forum. Fire and flame are connected with life and health, mirroring physically as body-heat, and with spiritual energy. (2) The Indic tribes know fire as Agni, a divine messenger who conveys prayers and sacrifices to the gods. Loosely, this could relate to the smith whose sparks fly into heaven creating the stars.

By the seiðr-road, that which is seen at night played a far more significant role to our ancestors then our current daytime focus. Perhaps this reflects how modern humans have turned away from the inner reality, that which is real, to an outer reality, that which is ever changing and uncertain. If so, all the more reason for those whose interests lie in this area to focus exclusively on seiðr - on the penetration of Wyrd consciousness - to aid the folk in their return to the Folksoul.

Reference
(1) Casting her right hand. Sunna's southerly direction is indicated by her 'right hand'; this is considered an Indo-European model. Comparatively, in Old and Modern Irish, *dess* and *deas* mean "south" and "right hand"; specifically lam des, "right hand", as opposed to lam cle, "left hand". The former being considered 'right, just, agreeable, well-arranged.' Reference: *Irish Folk Collection*, MS, *Lough Gur and Knockainey*; 1972.

(2) Spiritual energy. Having a 'fire in the head', or, Odin's eye in the well representing fire and water (a form of ice).

~ ~ ~

Vol.4: *Buri's grandsons [then] raised-up the flatland to be seen, fashioning the praiseworthy [and glorious] Midworld. Sun shone from the south, warming the hearthstones, and the ground became overgrown with green garden leeks [[garlic]].*

Buri's grandsons raised-up the flatland to be seen, fashioning the praiseworthy [and glorious] Midworld. Buri means "producer; inhabitant", he is the offspring of Aurgelmir and Audhumla, being licked from a block of salt, a salt lick. This compound signifies nourishment and purification, wisdom and knowledge. It is the subconscious mind, the third element of creation, or spiritual synthesis. Buri is that which is united through disintegration and separated through joining. He is the energy of Solve et Coagula, and the sum total of his ancestry - of his 'grandparents', Fire and Ice, and of his parents, Primal Tone of Ascension That Begins and Ends With Silence. From Buri comes perhaps the first mystic metaphor: salt of the earth. (1) Buri, like salt in abundance, had two children: Bor and Bestla.

Buri's grandsons are Óð, Vili, and Ve, the energies of soul, sense, and motion-hue, or Soul, Mind, and Body. Utilizing Aurgelmir's entire form to create Midworld is significant for the fledgling seiðu - his flesh becomes land, his blood becomes rivers and seas, his bones become stones, and his skull the sky itself. From experience: body-earth is the vehicle of understanding; blood-rivers-ocean, the means of sacrifice, is both the beginning and end of all endeavors; bone-stone is the seed of life, as seen in its marrow (to break a bone is to hinder forward-birth or reincarnation); skull-sky is that which survives, the truth of truth, the ultimate receptacle of transformation.

Bor and Bestla are etymologically linked with 'hole' and 'woody fiber', respectively. A hole has two energy weavings - one of fertility and the other of an opening - specifically from one realm of existence to another. Therefore, Bor is the gateway that teaches-releases expert seiðfolk from Urlag, or the gateway to crossover from spatial to non-spatial existence, from temporal to non-temporal existence.

Bestla's energy is that of a food-conducting fiber, such as seen in flax or hemp, both being used in the weaving of rope, baskets, and hair. Therefore, she exhibits a primal weaving. Flax is a lovely plant that exudes the energy of prosperity, lineage, and is linked to mid-summer tides. As the 'L' rune its attributes range from health and beauty to spiritual invisibility, to the comprehension of morality and to understanding the weavings of the ancients. (2) Consideration should also be given to the 'spear and spindle', or the 'linen and leek', a runo that brings together the energies of a man and woman.

Many years ago this seiðr scholar became particularly fond of a Pagan chant: *Cauldron of Changes, Blossom of Bone, Arch of Eternity, Hole in the Stone.* Combined, Bor and Bestla, as 'hole' and 'woody fiber', could easily represent the holed stones used in warp-weight looms.

Flax was well known to the Indo-Europeans who knew her as Uma, the Goddess of Flax, or the Goddess of Blue Flowers; and Mokosh, from Slavic myth, is a flaxen earth goddess of fertility and midwifery. As the "Moist Mother Earth" she spins flax and wool, the threads of life and death. Like Frau Holda, she is the guardian of housework and women's duties; she is often pictured flanked by two horsemen while standing next to a birch tree (mannaz and berkana, respectively). As hemp, Bestla would represent intoxication, purification, and the ability to overcome dark forces. From a Scythian tomb, the border design on a rug depicts a horseman approaching a goddess holding a 'tree of life', a hemp plant. (3) Hemp has a long history as a medicinal and sacred herb. During the

Inquisition for example, anyone using hemp, 'spiritually, medicinally, or otherwise' was persecuted as a witch.

The Indo-Europeans consider hemp a holy plant, a 'weed of wisdom', and a gift from the gods, for the 'welfare of mankind'; a divine herb said to bring about good health, long life, and visions of the gods. A favored drink of Indra, Hindu god of rain and thunder - who shared it with humanity to 'elevate consciousness' - hemp is considered a 'source of happiness', so that humans could 'take delight in the world'. Further, as a 'joy giver' and 'liberator', it made its users 'free from fear'. (4) Siva, a Hindu Supreme Being, is said to have sat under a hemp plant, achieving complete and inseparable union, and from Buddhist lore Siddhartha is said to have lived on nothing but hemp seeds for six years prior to discovering the truths of his philosophy; both, akin perhaps to Odin's diet of mead alone. As can be seen, 'grass' certainly has an open-ended energy weaving; and for seiðus, hemp is a significant aid in meditative states, bringing about deep insight and heightened awareness.

Midworld is just as it sounds, the world between. There exist 'buffers' 'above and below' Midworld, shielding it, so to speak, from the Over- and Underworlds. The shield 'above', before reaching the Overworld, is Alfheim; immediately above that and on an equal energy footing is Wanaheim and Ensigart. Above this all is Muspelsheim. The shield 'below', before reaching the Underworld, is Svartalfheim; immediately below that and on an equal energy footing is Jotunheim and Helheim. Below this all is Niflheim. For the amateur seiðu it is important to remember that direction is relative. Above and below, left and right, even such seemingly solid ideas as day and night are without time, space, or event.

Sun shone from the south, warming the hearthstones. In the northern hemisphere, around Sol Huel or the "Sun's Wheel" (Yule), the sun rises in the southeast and sets in the southwest. This passage indicates that Midworld took shape during the Midnight Sun, which would mark this tide as one of new beginnings. Warming the hearthstones is yet another knowledge-gem of seiðr: the hearth is symbolic of the domestic sun or the home, the cohesion of male and female, of love and harmony.

..and the ground became overgrown with green garden leeks [[garlic]]. Two times, in the last four strophes, green growing things are mentioned. The leek, in particular has a long northern European history. With the daffodil it is the national symbol of Wales and represents springtime. The

30

Old Icelandic word here is *lauki* and *laukr* ("leek; garlic") which is akin to Northern Germanic *laur* and *laukar*, meaning "flow out" and "leek; grow up", respectively. From 350 ACE, a woman's funerary urn bears the word *linalaukazf*, which has been rendered, 'linen (flax)-leek-prosperity.' Like hemp, flax and leek have medicinal and magical qualities; in particular, from *Flateyarbók* there exists an account of a cult object - a 'god' - that is wrapped in linen and preserved with leeks and herbs. This devise is passed among those gathered with each folk reciting a stanza of verse over it. (5)

Garlic and monkshood have long been used to repel darkness or adversity. Like the onion and leek, garlic is affected by moon phases. Of note for student seiðus who seek to access inner herbal knowledge: garlic grows during the moon's wane. Additionally, the ancient Iranians grew seven medicinal and magical herbs - garlic was one of them.

For seiðus interested in herb lore, here then are four to ponder from Heathen Lore: leek, flax, garlic, and hemp-cannabis. Their energy weavings are an open field for both research and application-exploration.

References

(1) Mystic metaphor. Coined phrase by the author to denote a figure of speech that belies a mystic meaning.

(2) Weavings of the ancients. Laguz, like all runes, have many aspects: flesh, heart, spirit, and ancestors, respectively in the example given.

(3) Hemp plant. Reference: *Frozen Tombs of Siberia*; S. Rudenko; 1953; throughout.

(4) Free from fear. Reference: *Atharva Veda* (throughout) lists hemp as one of the "five kingdoms of herbs", for it releases humans from anxiety.

(5) Verse over it. Reference: *Thunder - A Journal Dedicated to the Thunder Gods of Northern Europe*; 1999, twelfth issue.

~ ~ ~

Vol.6: *Then went the ruling powers, [the decision makers], to their tranquil and proud stools of decision-making; the holy gods gathering in council. To Night and New Moon they gave names, Morning they named, and Mid-day as well; and Afternoon, and Evening, for the first and next years - [their ancient beginnings] - to be counted, [to trace their descent].*

Names are implicit of overall worth. The giving of names should never be happen chance. Modern name meanings have become obscured, with no memory of their mystical and spiritual energy, which explains why some choose 'spiritual names', in an attempt to realign their energy with inner or soul identity. Because names are conscious they reflect the soul's nature; without a name, nothing can exist. Once identified, a name touches the innate mægen of a thing, activating it, energizing its character, creating its structure, and therefore it's Wyrd. This is yet another mystery of Wyrd consciousness.

Night is the subconscious mind or that which we are not consciously aware of but is ever present and quite active. The Greeks, like our Northern European ancestors, felt that night preceded the creation of all things; or, in the beginning, there was only night. There are places on earth that have night for months on end, and in the northern climes moons influence on the tides empties entire bays. Here, animals are more active at night, hunting and eating, and as the sun rises they sleep. Little wonder the importance of night and moon to our northern European ancestors.

New Moon / Moon: Symbolically, the new moon represents birth, the first quarter is youth and the full moon is adulthood, the last quarter is old age and the dark moon represents death. Mani is the full moon, Nyi the new moon, and Nithi the waning moon; additionally, Mani was known as 'time teller'. (1) According to Julius Caesar's *Gallic War* (1.50), the Germanic tribes would not engage in battle before the new moon. And from Tacitus' *Germania* chapter 11, it is related that all assemblies occur "..when the moon changes, or is full: since they believe such seasons to be the most fortunate for beginning all transactions." Further it states, "Neither in reckoning of time do they count, like us, the number of days but that of nights."

Regarding runic lore, *Havamal* 136 recommends 'call[ing], summon[ing] the *moon*' to subdue 'feud, war, and derision'; and according to Briffault, "The *moon* was connected with the shamans and the *lunar crescent* was represented on their magic drums (Lapps)." And from the *Indiculus Superstitionun et Paganiarum, in Capitularia Regum Francorum,* an eighth century text that condemns "religious practices": "Women can exercise witchcraft by means of the *moon.*"

Morning is the sun's rise on a new day, a time of awakening and promise, of beginnings, youth, and rejuvenation.

The essence of *Night, Morning, Mid-Day, Afternoon,* and *Evening,* are seen in the five periods of 'day', and the five stages of the tree: seed, root, tree, branch, and fruit. Physically they are the five fingers of a hand, five toes on the foot, the four limbs and head, and the five common senses. Plus, they are the four directions and center.

Morning, Mid-Day, and Evening, exclusively, are symbols of synthesis: Awake, Dream, and Deep-Sleep; Fire, Sun, and Moon; Midworld, Overworld, and Underworld; Red, White, and Black; Spring, Summer, and Winter; Voice, Mind, and Breath; Communion, Awareness, and Trance; Hearth, Ancestors, and Seiðr; Ve, Vili, and Óð; by extension, Body, Mind, and Spirit, all respectively.

..for the first and next years - [their ancient beginnings] - to be counted, [to trace their descent]. From a seiðr perspective time is a myth; there simply is no beginning no middle and no end. Nor was there one creation, nor will there be any one end, what exists is one continuous flow. What time has become is a root assumption, meaning that it has become commonly accepted as a division of space; as such it symbolically appears as a turning wheel, a progressive tide, or a cyclic period. Time is circular, with a beginning and end, and has become convenient and comfortable; a natural progression that allows the bodymind to progress from one point, like birth, to another, like death. This arrangement has become both internal and external because it has become an endless source of fascination. Accordingly, our inner experience is translated in such terms, meaning: thoughts, words, and deeds have imprinted the bodymind with such ideas. This means that emotional-intellectual experience has become woven in such a way to give the impression of sequence. Think on this: does time slow down or speed up? Logically the answer is 'no', yet these ideas manifest as both personal perception and figures of speech (power of a name). Would-be seiðus must understand that existence is more than neurological eruption.

For a moment consider the concept of time as a wheel; once done, see how this wheel - like all wheels - has the ability to move forward and back. If, therefore, time can be expressed as the Wheel of the Year, or 'time marching on', can it not also be logically deduced that rolling and marching can take place in any direction? Likewise, this wheel has a rim-outer, with spokes-middle, attached to a hub-inner. This middle passage way then - traveling the spokes so to speak - allows access to all of time, space, and matter - which, in turn, explains the free-wheeling movement and true nature of evolution.

In truth, all time - 'past', 'present', and 'future' - exists simultaneously; or, the concept of linear time is inaccurate. Seconds, minutes, days, months, and years are not consecutive moments or events, not things that happen to you, but what is expected based on personal conclusions. What separates these things, what gives them depth and duration, space and span, is personal perception; 'past', 'present', and 'future' are the psychic organization of experience.

Consider the choices you make, consider that each is a strand of time with the possibility of manifesting in unknowable ways (after all, when has anything turned out exactly as you expected). If this is possible to visualize then the manner in which time can be manipulated should flicker into your imagination. This exercise shows how any choice made materializes as its own unique beginning of time, space, and matter, as a new door of awareness, a different course of action, a new opportunity. With this either firmly or loosely grasped, consider this: the moment you have a thought it begins to change, being tempered by events of the 'past' and ideas of the 'future', equally as it is affected by every following 'present' moment thoughts.

Back to linear versus spatial time: reincarnation, for example, can occur in any 'direction'. This means that your next life may occur in what appears to you now as 'past'; equally as a 'future'-you could be re-born into a 'present'-you. The concept of being born and dying appear as waves of radical change to your waking reality, which can be perceived as either joyous or traumatic events depending on personal perception, but to the greater mind, to consciousness, such events are barely a ripple. An immediate example would be how a sight or sound or smell - an activation of the senses - can 'take you back' so that a 'past' memory is relived, including all the happiness or sadness that originally existed. In that moment the 'past' journeys to the 'present'; likewise, the 'present' can respond to 'future' events, with their full experience being relived-felt-experienced. Now, these are not isolated events, they occur frequently, daily, often without being consciously noticed. Obviously the mind is perfectly capable of such events, or else they would not occur. In fact, currently, at this very moment, you are living multiple lives, but your bodymind is currently only focused on one. Freshman seiðus must understand that all barriers are self-imposed and that focus must be fine-tuned. Simply put, this then is the flowing manner of Wyrd consciousness.

These examples go towards explaining the nature of prophecy, for example, and why answers appear either vague or wrong. Free will is the nature of being and exists to alter any experience regardless of when it occurs. Do not consider the thread of existence to come only from birth to present moment, again - this is linear thought. Instead, see an imaginably vast expanse filled with threads that criss-cross in every direction. If viewed, these threads go on 'forever', having no beginning or end. Physical existence, the bodymind, sees but a small section of this vast loom. The Over- and Underworlds, for example, exist from different 'angles' within this loom. Imagine three or more folk looking at this vast loom from different directions, some would view it from 'above', being taller for example, some would view it from 'below', being shorter, others would view it with disinterest, not caring for weaving or looms, others would be fascinated in the mechanism, and others in the artistry. Though there is but one loom there are many perspectives, each tempered by emotive experience. Now see this loom as containing many smaller looms, like fruit adorning branches. These smaller looms are individual souls. Now see these small looms with smaller looms inside of them, or see the larger loom as being but a smaller loom in an ineffable loom. Most souls journey along a single thread, from a pre-determined beginning and ending based on personal understanding of the ordering of things (time, space, and matter). While other souls learn to 'skip' across the threads, following alternate threads to other destinations or conclusions. Now, for the adept seiðu, this image has long been removed; seeing clearly they know there are no looms, there are no threads, there is only Wyrd consciousness, or the deftly flowing movement of energy currents.

Now - and again for beginning seiðus - this is how journeys are completed, by 'grasping' time. Follow the thread to either 'past' or 'future'. Travel on inner realms is not the same as travel on Midworld, which is primarily upon the surface from one point in space to another. Instead of traveling forward or back on the Wheel of Time, its Center must be penetrated so that time and space, both, can be transcended. The Tivar do indeed exist, though not in terms commonly understood; they are organized energy weavings, they exist adjacent to Midworld at all times. Visiting them, therefore, is simply a matter of leaping the barrier of time and space. Just as the Norns 'cut' the threads of existence, using scissors - the twin blades of psychic and emotional communication - to slice through physical existence-coordinates.

Unlike Indic ideas of reincarnation, where time is linear, that one life is lived after another, in sequence over the course of time, the Northern European model - from an advanced seiðr perspective - views all of existence as occurring within the current moment. (2) There is no 'bad karma' that causes suffering or any 'good karma' that assures ample fortune. This explains how we are our deeds, or that which we do now - in this moment - is what we are now, in this moment. If life is simultaneous then every 'present' presents an opportunity for right action - in every direction - to change or make right what brings about discomfort. Naturally, such virtues as self-reliance and self-responsibility take on new meanings in that all experience is open-ended; or, there exists the ability to alter both 'past' and/or 'future' events. For the working seiðu, this is a matter of re-weaving the loom of life, of restructuring the tapestry of existence.

For example, fate is predetermined in that all deeds done are the accumulation of all experiences. Each individual predetermines their fate based on previous accomplishments and re-actions, previous attainments and capacities, previous culture and education, previous grounding and preparation, previous training and upbringing - in all previous circumstances, or courses of action-choice. Powerful seiðus realize the importance of rethinking this very moment, immediately, so that the 'future' no longer follows a prescribed pattern. For those who seek to learn seiðr, this must be understood: before repeating a tendency or impulse or any expected response or routine reply, consider instead a course never taken, a route yet explored, the deeds not yet sung. This is how master seiðus change the 'past' – accustomed or predictable decisions – to re-weave fate. Wyrd is decided in advance based on a predisposition to act, respond, or reply in a specific manner that has been habitually relied upon. Seiðus do not control the flow of Wyrd, but dive directly into its profound current.

Health as well is not limited by time in that even cells have cognitive ability, however, just as the bodymind has convinced itself of a beginning and end, this information has been 'given' to the cells, so that they ever renew with the 'idea' of: slow metabolism, increasing aches and pains, loss of strength and stamina, and eventual death. Precognition, for example, is 'thinking ahead' so that when a change needs be made the 'future' sends a message to its 'present', or 'past', in the form of an idea or course of action, so that at the cellular level, effective change comes about. Now, because free will exists, the 'present' can choose to ignore this 'future' advice, so that no physical, mental, psychological, or psychic change occurs in accord to the 'future' suggestion.

Even so, when the soul communicates there is no other option but to listen. The bodymind receives this signal when it is tuned-in or living in accord with nature; or in harmony-center-balance. Mostly however, the bodymind is preoccupied with physical-mechanical existence, so the message is often garbled or confused. Guidance from the soul then is unclear, causing frustration, among other things. Which is precisely what seiðus train for, sacrifice for and dedicate themselves towards: assist the folk in interpreting guidance from the Folksoul, from the Wellspring of Wyrd.

This thesis is maintained by dreams, specifically, the ability to lucid dream, which is identical to waking consciousness (or should be in an accomplished seiðu). Emotion and intellect are so associated with time that the only way many have of escaping from this self-created construct is through dreams, where reality seems to 'bend' or somehow not apply as you experience flight or breathing underwater, and other fantastical things. There is nothing that exists that is not energy or that does not display consciousness, including dreams and what are encountered in them. Dreams, the deep-mind, allow individual focus to expand, allowing an experience of expansion within time and space. Instead of having a narrow perspective of the bodymind alone, would-be seiðus must identify with the greater multiverse, which is to fully immerse them into the Well of Wyrd. Dreams allow you to access a vast wealth of information, for they are marvelous wells of creativity and inspiration. Once drank from these deep draughts release the natural-organic identity, which manifests in the ease in which life is dealt with, even the most traumatic events. In short, there are no problems only challenges. Dreams allow you to see around corners, so to speak.

Overall, apprentice seiðus must intimately understand core reality or else there will be no weaving within the Well, no experience of Wyrd consciousness. The purpose of life is, after all, to not endlessly repeat itself, struggling through lessons already learned.

References

(1) Waning moon. Reference: Thuleheim Knowledge Base. Specifically: *The Mothers, A Study of The Origins of Sentiments and Institutions*; R. Briffault; 1927; throughout. And, *The Sun Goddess, Myth, Legend, and History*; S. McGrath; 1997; page 147-152.

(2) Current moment. Reference: *What Becomes of the Soul After Death*; Sri Swami Sivananda; India; 1979.

~ ~ ~

[Interpolation and Vol.7] *Churning Well's whirlpool below, heaven's whirlpool above, Grotti is walked by nine maidens. World above, the Ensi met on the Whirling-Field, building stone alters in high places. They laid hearths, forged riches, wrought tongs and tools.*

The first sentence is an interpolation, the latter part strophe 7.

Grotti is the grinding millstone. (1) Progressing from a flat base stone with a handheld roundish stone, to a mortar and pestle, to a hand mill or turning-stone with a handle, to a rotary quern, to the water- and windmill, the millstone was a well-established image, tool, and daily task for our ancestors. In every example, the lower unmoving portion represents earth while the upper moving implement was seen as revolving sky above, leaving its central hole as a symbol of fertility. Seiðr-wise, Grotti is the mobility and constancy of Over-, Under-, and Midworld, while its unmoving and primal center - the Pole Star - is the axis around which all existence revolves. (2) For skilled seiðus this opening allows entrance and egress from one world to another.

This hole, energy-wise, relates to the portals found across the worlds. There exist places on Midworld where Ley-lines criss-cross, which are the naturally occurring electro-magnetic energy currents of the planet. (3) Where these energy lines cross there exist levels of intensity that often manifest as whirlpools or openings that allow passage, in many directions, to many realms of existence. Similar lines are seen in a weaving pattern, where the warp and weft cross, and their point of contact always a strengthening of the whole. These openings are called portals and they are means in which powerful seiðus escape the temporariness of Midworld for the greater awareness of other realms of consciousness, or the penetration of all energies simultaneously. For once a seiðus is able to access this energy center all movement ceases, they are then able to bound-bind, rebound-rebind, or unbound-unbind; meaning, they move from being moved to being a mover. Grotti then is the center of all centers, the root of all roots.

While traversing the multiverse a seiðu may encounter a 'black hole', which serves, much like a portal, as an entrance-exit point. Exclusively, black and white holes in space are coordinate points on which a well-versed seiðu can chart a course across time, space, and event.

Like most wheel-shaped objects, Grotti's surface can be divided into sections; either nine sections, to denote the nine maidens, or a circle with an equal armed cross that, spinning, would more rightly resemble a multi-armed swastika. In that it churns-turns the waters below and the heaven-stars above, Grotti could be the significator of time itself. The nine maidens - who walk-rotate its surface - could then be the nine passages of time or nine seasonal changes-progressions of the stars across the sky. Further still, these nine divisions could represent the nine runos given to Heimdallr, the ones he taught to humanity. Runos possibly sung to him as a child - much like Groa relates healing and protective runes to her son - gifts that are passed from parent to child, from mouth to ear.

From *Kalevala* comes the Sampo, a great millstone that produces the "bear-stars" and the "solar disk", as well as vast amounts of wealth, which are secured with nine locks. (4)   These locks could be, energy-wise, similar to the nine maidens mentioned in *Grotta's Song* who turn the Great Mill; and what appear to be star references indicate what archeology is ever confirming - that our ancestors were well versed in the movements of stars, planets, and the like. Something all three of these powerful symbols have in common - the World Tree, Grotti, and the Sampo - are that they all have three 'roots'. (5)   Symbolic of a tripod-triskel, these three aspects could represent body, mind, and soul (among other trinities).   Other striking similarities can perhaps be drawn to Charlemagne's destruction of the Irminsul and the 'felling' of Aurgelmir. (6)

The words *eyluthr* and *luthr* are used to describe what becomes of Aurgelmir at his death; they mean 'island' and 'box mill', respectively. After Aurgelmir's blood was released, a great flood ensued, the only survivor of which was Bergelmir; but Snorri's translation that this brought about the death of Bergelmir is incorrect (and certainly that Bergelmir may somehow relate as a Norse Noah). Instead of killing Bergelmir - who is the endnote of creation, so must survive to sing the final death knell -

the Great Mill saved his life when he and his family climbed upon it to escape the deluge of his father's blood.

The multiverses are revolved by Grotti's turning and so become the source of all nourishment and wealth, all abundance and plenty. From *Vafthruthnismal*, Mundilfoeri, father of Sun and Moon, is the turner of Grotti; symbolically 'turning; marking' the passage of time - or the processional march of the equinoxes and solstices - which makes him the Great Time Keeper, or keeper of all time. (7) Always spooling back to Grotti - like thread around a distaff - is the idea of world axis and point around which the heavens revolve-evolve. A theme so firmly rooted in Heathenry's Folksoul that Ælfric - a 10th century English prose writer, monk, lexicographer, and Abbot of Eynsham - wrote in his *Sermones Catholici* that the water mill equates with the three realms of existence, namely, heaven, earth, and hell. Saint James, from a 14th century painting, is depicted as the great heavenly wheel turner (a later Mundilfoeri?), and from the same period an illumined manuscript depicts the great heavenly wheel being turned by two angels - perhaps Fenja and Menja reincarnated.

Heimdallr is said to be the son of nine giant women "at the edge of earth", and resides at Himinbjorg, or "Sky Mountain". (8) Exclusively, Tiw is the Pole Star around which Grotti revolves and Heimdallr the great mountain range on earth that lies beneath him. Perhaps a reference to the cosmic mountains of Indo-European and Uralic traditions: Dharmagiri in Sanskrit, meaning "Mountain of (Cosmic) Law" (also known as Kailish and Meru); Belukha and Kurgurka, the "Sacred Three Peaks"; and "Glass Mountain", respectively.

As related in strophe 2, the "nine tree-women of the measuring-tree", could be Heimdallr's mothers. Often translated as 'nine trees' or 'nine mothers' or 'nine branches', the latter sounds similar to how circumpolar shamans access the Nine Worlds: by walking up nine steps on a tree, or passing through nine tree branches decorated with colorful ribbons to represent the different realms. Other references of nine women come from *Preiddeu Annwfn*, or The Spoils of Annwfn, where a cauldron is kindled by the "breath of nine maidens" on the island of Caer Sidi, a rotating fortress, part of the Fortunate Isles of Celtic Lore, ruled by nine maidens-sisters.

Another excellent example of nine women is the nine black-clad *disir* or *fylgjur*, and the same number dressed in white, of the Icelandic

Flateyjarbok and *Brennu-Njals saga,* which represent the luck, well-being, and fertility of the sippe-tribe. These Disir are 'fairy godmothers' (so to speak) who, like the Norns, oversee a child at birth, assuring they are rightly gifted.

Cosmic centers the world over are also associated with cosmic serpents: Nidhogg and the Lambton Worm on Midworld, and Cadus and Caput Draconis in the heavens, for example. Jörmungandr means 'earth wand' so could represent another symbol of a turning-rod or axis mundi. 'Nine' and 'serpents' both are mentioned in the Old English *Nine Herbs Charm,* specifically, "Woden took nine glory-twigs and struck the adder so that it flew into nine parts." The *Havamal* 137 relates how Odin hung on the World Tree for nine nights, bringing forth the runes. These nine nights are often equated to a woman's nine months of pregnancy which brings forth a child - certainly the greatest of all treasures - but how did a man become linked to this? More to the point perhaps is Odin's ring Draupnir which produces eight additional rings every ninth night, perhaps connecting him to the division of the year, which, in turn, could be depicted as three interlocking triangles (either Hrungnir's Heart or the Valknot). (9)

Nine is certainly a well-established number of completions, or that all the worlds are complete and self-contained, meaning in this regard: the Heathen worldview is such that there exists no need to search elsewhere or when. (10)

Vol.7: *The Ensi met on the Whirling-Field, building stone altars in high places. They laid hearths, forged riches, wrought tongs and tools.*

This is strophe 7, which has been added at the end of an interpolation.

The war gods met on the *Whirling-Field,* symbolic of all world evolution, or Grotti. They build *stone altars* on high, but to whom? Alters - as representatives of the divine center - are the middle-points between heaven and earth, so this strophe seems to relate a spiritual center, or place of all-wisdom. This horgr then, intuitively, contains the seed-stones of tradition, where heritage and inheritance are nourished and allowed to grow. Afterwards they established hearths and forges, meaning, home and love coupled with superiority and control.

References

(1) Grinding millstone. There are several Finno-Scandian references to millstones, including *Kalevala*, *Skáldskarpamál*, and *Grottasöngr*, for example.

(2) Midworld. Grotti is mentioned by Egil Skallagrimson, referenced in *Skáldskarpamál*, *Grotta's Song*, and *Kalevala*; some references list two giantesses as turners: Fenja and Menja.

(3) Currents of the planet. Reference: *The Old Straight Track*; A. Watkins; London; 1962; entire book subject.

(4) Sampo. Possibly from Sanskrit skambha, or "prop, post, pillar", a 'tree-trunk' that is both the world axis and the circular-celestial plane that encircles the world. From *Artharva Veda*, the skambha is that which conglomerates all systems, from 'smallest' to 'largest', so that atoms create stones, which create rocks, which form earth. Skambha is the precursor of the complex-physical world whose essence defines all of existence. The grinding-turning of skambha creates heat that spreads as waves of water through the universe. As the central pillar it is un-decaying and has three layers, the 'below', 'middle', and 'above'. A great snake, Shesha, sleeps next to it and awakens only when the heat-waters rise or threaten to sink the middle realm of existence (where humans live). Shesha is time and his turnings are viewed as ages or precessions of heaven, earth, and the under realm; equinoxes and solstices are examples of Shesha's processions, therefore, cyclic time. Skambha's turning, or 'three scaffolds', represents the zenith, nadir, and zone formed by the tilt in its axis (the celestial tropics). Shesha, as world serpent, is beneficial to humans in that he supports the earth on which they live.

(5) Three roots. Earth, Mountain, and Sea, which are similar to the Celto-Germanic "land, sea, and sky."

(6) 'Felling' of Aurgelmir. Irminsul relates to the World Tree like Aurgelmir relates to Grotti.

(7) Mundilfoeri. Meaning, 'time, remember - convey, mark', or 'to remember the passage of time.'

(8) At the edge of earth. Reference: *Völuspá hin skamma*.

(9) Theosophic reduction. Eight multiplied by nine is seventy-two, which becomes nine by theosophic reduction. Further, if 366 (traditional lunar calculation for number of days in a year) were divided by 8 (the additional rings produced by Draupnir), this would equal 45.75, which is the number of days between the eight divisions of the year; or, the solstices, equinoxes, and cross-quarter days.

(10) Completions. Reference: *Symbols of Transformation*, Jung, C.G., London, 1956; and, *Studies in Symbology*, R.A. Lidstone, New York, 1997. Both references are throughout.

~ ~ ~

Vol.8: *They played at tables, glad and cheerful were they, and there was no lack of gold. Until three giants came from Jotunheim on matters relating to marriage, very loathsome they were to the Ensi.*

They played at tables. Games carry two symbols: first as an attempt to win over others, such as through a social position, and second as an attempt to win over self, or the act of individuation. Tables therefore would be an opportunity for action and contemplation.

..matters relating to marriage. The Ensi are sublime and illumined energy patterns, whereas the *three giant* maids represent primal matter seeking growth or evolution. Exclusively, the Ensi did not want to mix their force with Jotunic form, something the Wana had no qualm with (a union perhaps that created a greater understanding of Wyrd consciousness among them, strengthening their seiðr practice).

The first two lines of Völuspá 9 are identical with the first two lines of Völuspá 6, clearly an interpolation, as are the next eight strophes, commonly referred to as the 'catalogue of dwarfs', which do not concern this verse commentary. After this, strophe 17 begins with the word "until" indicating a missing section, suggesting that a verse, or more, are missing here; one/s that may or may not relate the marriage-merging matters mentioned above.

~ ~ ~

Vol.17: *Then came three together - of the rare host - powerful and loved Ensi out of their enclosure. They found on land, light of availing might, Ask and Embla, loose of the thread of life.*

43

What prompted the Ensi to come out of their *enclosure*, and why was their appearance so rare? Was an ultimatum given from the three giant maidens, demanding these Overworld gods merge-share their light-blood with the other multiverse energies? In doing so, perhaps, both sides coming together to create a new race: humans. Speculatively, why would the Ensi be resistant to participate, why would they decide to create humans alone, without the aid of Jotuns, or of dwarves? Is it sure the Ensi did not join the Jotuns to create humans? With missing strophes these questions cannot be know with surety. Of note, the response was three for three, Jotuns and Ensi.

Three is the number of spiritual synthesis, so if the two groups were to join, working together to bring forth humans, their number would be six, which is the representation of ambivalence and equilibrium. This would signify a merging of the Overworld with the Underworld for the creation of Midworld, which did in fact take place when earth was sculpted from Aurgelmir's body.

Ask and Embla. Two trees from which were formed the first man and woman, respectively. Their energy is akin to Lifthrasir and Lif, another couple, who, during Ragnarök, will seek shelter inside the World Tree. Living off dew they will survive to repopulate earth with human energy. The ancestry of humans to trees is unique to ancient Europe, and of this novice seiðus should take note.

..light of availing might .. loose of the thread of life. There exists within these two enough animating principle to keep them alive, but nothing to demarcate them as humans, their next evolutionary step.

~ ~ ~

Vol.18: *They had no inhaling breath, no soul, nor had they inherited a noble mind, no blood or warm voice, no good color or moral. Inhaling Breath gave Óð, Noble Mind gave Hoenir, Blood and Warm Voice gave Lodur, and good hue.*

Three threads entwined create soul: inhaling breath, noble mind, blood and voice. Óð-Oth, Oth-Hoenir, La-Lodur: othila / othila, laguz - success and happiness, contentment and poise, harmony and ancestry, appreciation and recognition, coupled with health and beauty, vitality and inner truth, morality and deep understanding. (1) These are the birth gifts of humans.

Regarding the double othila, this rune can be seen in the Troll Cross, an iron amulet worn by early Scandinavians. It was thought to protect the wearer from harm or dark energy, which is why it was worn and carved onto objects - such as buildings, cradles, and barns - to protect property, children, and animals, respectfully.

What if there were three more gifts, ones given by the Jotun maidens? Suggestively, these would be: existence, structure, and potential. After all, there is no shape-form present in the gifts of the Ensi, no appearance or likeness. Therefore, did the Ensi simply create warm-blooded and intelligent trees? If so, the Jotun maiden's gifts of existence, structure, and potential would be vital for humans to take on a form akin to that of their sculptors.

If the Ensi did exclude the three maidens, then they omitted primal-animal nature, and like the fairy godmother of lore who feels overlooked, these three could have brought a curse rather than a blessing. Or, by not marrying-merging with Jotun-subconsciousness, the Ensi-consciousness failed to gift the first pair with centeredness and harmonious relatedness. Either way, there does exist within humans a sense of limitation and barrier, a sense of forgetfulness that causes humans to be ignorant of their divine heritage, leaving them to forever quest externally instead of seeking self within.

Based on personal experience and insight this seiðr scholar has perceived six gifts given: three from the Ensi and three from the Jotun-Wana. (2) The Jotunic gifts are:

Existence-life:
- ævi, which is 'age, time'; and
- fjöl, which is 'much, multitude, increase'.
Additionally, this latter would include:
- fjöl-höfðaðr, or 'many-headed';
- fjöl-kunnigr, or 'skilled in magic';
- fjöl-kyngi, or 'witchcraft, wizardry';
- fjöl-kyngisfólk, or 'wizard folk, magic art, sorceress, witch'; and
Being completed with:
- líf-life, or lífaðr, which is 'full of life'; líf-dagar, which is 'life-days, life.
These gifts represent great age and great numbers-offspring, well thinking and skill in magic, full of life and seeking life. Algiz, Fehu, Laguz.

Structure-form:
- lík, which is 'living body';
- mynd, which is 'shape, form, image, same manner'; and
- vöxtr, which is 'growth, increase, productive' (vöxtuligr, is 'big, great size').

These gifts represent living body and shapely form, growth, and the ability of growth. Mannaz and Wunjo.

Potential-promise:
- heit, which is 'solemn promise, vow'; and
   - heita, which is 'give a name to, call on one, to plight one's faith to, vow one's person to another, betrothed to one', (also: heita, heitta, heittr, or 'to heat', 'to brew', and 'brewing').

These gifts represent a promise to come when called - to appear when invoked, to be trothed one to another - plus knowledge of brewing, or intoxication of the soul. Hagalaz.

As such, the Jotun runic gifts could be: Algiz, Fehu, Laguz, Mannaz, Wunjo, and Hagalaz. Representing: exploration and comprehension, prophecy and intuition, evolution and harmony (Algiz); unification and harmony with all worlds (Fehu); health and beauty, inner wisdom, comprehension and morality, understanding of the ancients (Laguz); force, sensation, and comprehension (Mannaz); endurance and gaiety, art and transmission of messages through air, increase of intellect, incarnational knowledge and cognition (Wunjo); and, understanding and application, trance and inspiration, knowing the origin of all things (Hagalaz). Assuredly, these are aspirations for seiðus, equally as they are possibilities for all folk.

Regarding Óð, Hoenir, and Lodur - as soul, mind, and body, respectively, their attributes are twined:
- Óð is cojoined with æthem, which is human breath and vital air;
- Hoenir is cojoined with Mimir, who is conscious mind and divine mind; and
- Lodur is cojoined with lyke, which is sacred fruitfulness and physical-tree form, or human relationship to the World Tree.

References
(1) Deep understanding. Based on the author's understanding of runic energy.

(2) Jotun-Wana. Representing an alliance not a relation.

~ ~ ~

Vol.19: *I know a Yew that stands, Yggdrasil it is called, a high tree sprinkled with white clay, and there comes the dew - marking the tree - falling from the open river valley. It stands evergreen above Urd's Well.*

..Yew that stands, Yggdrasil. There is a long-standing debate over the exact species of the World Tree. Seiðr-wise, all trees have World Tree energy, however, of the two primary choices - Ash and Yew - evidence leans to the latter. Perhaps the confusion stems from Old Norse *barraskr*, or "needle ash", which means yew tree. Surely, both were highly regarded but if the facts were weighed, the yew would prove to have a distinct advantage. Its ancient origins, pronounced longevity, evergreen leaves, the safety of birds and deer in its presence, and the ability to induce trance are some of the items discussed in this section.

Yews are native to Ireland, Britain, and Scandinavia, equally as they are to Syria, Iran, the Caucasus region, and the Himalayas. They thrive in chalky soil, as is the case in southern England, or limestone, in Scotland - which is one of the clues, or how the Norns kept the World Tree whole with the addition of 'white clay'.

They are slow growing and long-lived trees. A beautiful example is the Fortingall Yew - said to be 3,000 to 5,000 years old - which is considered the geographic and spiritual center of Scotland. Not far from its venerable branches is a Bronze Age carn, the Mount of the Dead, or Carn nam Marbh, and next to this is Duneaves, or, the House of Nemed, indicating a sacred grove. Counting trunk rings on a yew to determine age does not apply because some simply stop growing, going dormant for many years. Then, uniquely, the yew may regenerate itself by growing a new trunk within an old one. This ability to rejuvenate itself, even if injured or seemingly dead, lends an aura of immortality.

Yews have a long and straight trunk with branches that spread to create a beautiful woven canopy. From its sides it seeps a white sap (perhaps a secondary reference to 'white clay'), and has a red-orange to purple wood, similar to the color of blood. They are hardy, durable, and have narrow stiff leaves that form a spiral pattern around each branch, which ends in blunt spear-like points. The arils on female yews are known as 'acorns', 'apples', or 'nuts', which accounts for the kenning: 'Tree With Three

Fruits'. This indicates that references to an Oak tree, Apple tree, or Hazel tree (respectively), could easily relate back to a yew.

When pollinating, generally February and March, yews deposit large amounts of yellow dust over a vast area, lending to their reputation of generating abundance and profundity. The Forest of Dean and the New Forest in England, as well as the Cuilgeagh Mountains of Northern Ireland, are all areas containing entire yew groves, so are excellent places to watch this enchanting phenomenon.

All yews are poisonous, yet, their berries are safely eaten by thrushes, waxwings, and other birds; while cows and horses that nibble its leaves are often found dead nearby. Deer love its foliage and eat it freely and safely, which relates to the Lore's reference of hart-stags who feed upon the World Tree. However, these poisonous properties effect more than animals. Caesar, in his *Gallic Wars*, chapter VI relates how Catuvolcus, Chieftain of the Eburones, committed suicide by taking a yew extract. Aside from its dangers, yew is also medicinal, and from a highly skilled seiðr perspective: it has the ability to harm or heal. Traditionally it has been used by trained herbalists for the treatment of rheumatism and epilepsy, liver ailments, snakebites and rabies, and as an abortifacient. Currently, the National Cancer Institute of America is researching yew's primary substance, taxol, to halt the division-growth of cancer cells. Preliminary tests have shown results effective in breast, ovarian, and lung cancers (intuitively, centers of nurturing, reproduction, and vital breath).

Throughout Europe yews and churchyards are seemingly synonymous, which explains their kenning of 'graveyard tree' (considering the longevity of these trees it is easy to imagine which came first; or, that yews were considered the first 'churches' or places of congregation). The residents of Selborne, England had an amazing example of a graveyard tree when their local yew was blown over during Windstorm Vivian in 1990. Found within its tangled root ball (growing in St. Mary's churchyard) were the skulls and bones of over 30 bodies. Contrary to how this may appear, the local inhabitants considered this event quite regular, affirming their notion of the yew as a "Tree of Life."

Yew wood is often found in bogs and archaeological sites, its wood well known as sturdy yet pliable, knot free and straight growing, laced with intricate patterns. Both practical and ornamental objects were and are crafted from yew, such as spears and dagger handles, farming tools, axles and wheels, mead kegs and mill cogs, pins and pulleys, furniture and sculpture, lutes, bowls and drinking tankards. (1)   An English saying relates, "A post of yew will outlast a post of iron", and indeed, the Scandinavians made nails from yew wood for use in their sea-worthy longboats.   Also from Heathen lore, Ullr, God of the Longbow, lives in Ydalir or "Yew Dales".

The world's oldest wood weapon is a spear found in England that dates back 150,000 years.   Nor were yew toxins ignored in the making of weapons; arrow- and spearheads would have been dipped in a poisonous mix to assure a quick death.   Divining rods were ideally made of yew (other excellent choices being hazel and rowan).   Finally, yew can be used to create an excellent fire; however, considering its sacred connections, it is easy to imagine such flames had a divine focus.

Yews were often used as landmarks, boundaries markers, and 'witch posts' along roads and other byways; known for their durability, this makes perfect sense.   The *Battle of Mag Mucrama*, or the Yew Tree of the Disputing Sons, relates the Irish tale of two tribes who fought over a single tree.   As symbols of continuity and emblems of ancestry, yews were thought to 'stand witness' and 'record in memory' all the events that transpired around them.

Indeed, yews have a strong presence about them - a deep impression of mystery that ripples through being - something quite perceptible upon entering a grove or standing near one.   Seiðr-wise this is their spiritual aura, their life-force, and it is brimming with abundance.   Stepping beneath their dark boughs the outer world seems to slowly fade, more than the cooler air and dim light, more than the muffled sound and accompanying stillness, the world takes on a distinct 'outside' and 'inside' feeling as you enter the yew's rich, deep-currented and conscious energy. This place is like no other.   Beyond a cave or grotto, a sacred grove or mountaintop, beneath these boughs is an intelligence that welcomes and elevates human vibrations, soothes emotions, eases stress, rids the bodymind of illness, and erases all fear.   No place else has this particular seiðu felt this - other then deep within and surrounded by peat bogs - the keen, intimate, and wondrous awareness called 'yew'.   For this reason, many wear yew about their neck, artfully crafted into medallions or rune shapes or fashioned into beads; an old custom is to keep yew sticks by a doorway to ward off evil.   Both are attempts to bring yew energy around and within.

Literature on the subject has long indicated the trance-inducing affect of yew, by simply sitting beneath it. On a hot day at Hermannsdenkmal in the Teutoburger Forest (above Detmold, Germany), this seiðu sat under a huge yew. The first impression received was how its needles formed a soft brown bed in a circle, like a perimeter. The temperature beneath-under was markedly cooler - sitting back, spine to the trunk, eyes closed, there came a new odour, an unfamiliar odour, and under that a current of 'something else'. Settling in and breathing deeply to still the heart that 'something else' entered the nostrils to pierce the skull and rest between and above the eyebrows. Immediately a sensation of lifting, literally elevation, entered the physical. Opening eyes, to assure location-direction, the world beyond these branches appeared green-tinted. Closing the eyes and continuing to breathe deeply - to allow soul's release into the seething - images began to flash all around, slow at first, describable, then faster. Though recognizable these images were moving at an incredible rate, soul was moving at an incredible rate, accelerating upwards until a piercing occurred. Awareness punctured transcendent consciousness, that layer of 'thick air', to rise and 'look' around from this new perspective. There were threads everywhere, everywhere coiling and knotting, coiling and un-knotting, vibrating and shimmering, 'singing' as they moved. There were threads of sun and moon and season, threads of All Worlds humming, threads of unwounding and of wells bubbling from deep no-where springs, and runos and life and death, and the tree - The Tree - consciousness incarnate. Its fruit, glistening Folksouls whose seeds were like stars upon unfathomable seas of undulating grass.

There was a golden woman there - huge and thick with 'loud' features - striding across an ocean of green vibrancy towards where this seiðus' soul peered out. From a distance she lifted this soul upwards and cradled it, singing into its being, causing it to soar onwards, rushing in all directions simultaneously, until there existed a firm surface beneath and behind that prompted the bodymind to open its eyes. And there I was, sitting beneath a yew tree.

There are many Irish tales where yews play prominent roles, such as: *The Wooing of Etaine, Tristan and Iseult,* and *The Exile of Conall Corc.* (2) Notably, we learn from these the importance of yews in ancient culture. For example, the Irish considered the yew to be the oldest being on earth, its wood was used to inscribe ogham upon - to include moon phases and law codes - its stakes were thought to separate the dead from each other or from the living, and that yews buried on a grave will take on the shape of the body beneath (this seiðr pilgrim has seen such a tree in the old East

Germany). Further, druids were said to toss handfuls of yew pollen upon a gathered clan, seemingly, a blessing to impart a sense of ancestry and lineage (yet another link of yews as gateways to otherworlds). (3)

The Celtic and Germanic tribes made sacred and enchanted objects from yew. The Greek goddess Hecate, one of the oldest triple divinities, who ruled 'heaven, earth, and the underworld', was said to sit beneath a yew at a crossroad (where three roads met). Yews were traditionally planted at well sites as 'guardians', and often decorated with bright colored ribbon and garlands of flowers throughout the year. There are twin yews at the Well of Glastonbury, standing between them this seiðr explorer discovered a whirling-vortex energy; and recent examination upon them has concluded they have been there since 300 ACE.

Eihwaz the rune and idho the ogham represent yew-sound motion and so impact the bodymind on a cellular level, and deeper still. The sound of yew in both systems, seiðr-wise, is: EOH, UR, and YR. All of which vibrate at a primal, stirring, seething level - prompting the roots within us. Then there is the sacred cow goddess IO, a triple energy giver of milk, whose stream flows as the Milky Way. Would you know more, and what?

It stands evergreen above Urd's Well. Urd is the first of the Norns named. She is existence, which is the connecting thread between humans and the Well, or primordial wisdom.

References
(1) Mead kegs. An Irish saying goes, "Yew is grave to the vine."

(2) Conall Corc. Reference: *A Guide to Irish Mythology*, D. Smyth, Dublin, 1988; page 89. *Celtic Heritage - Ancient Tradition in Ireland and Wales*, A. Rees and B. Rees, London, 1961; pages 176 & 186.

(3) Otherworlds. Reference: *Earth Rites*, J. and C. Bord, London, 1982, page 199.

~ ~ ~

Vol.20: *From there came maidens - being friendly and knowing much magic - three from the sea, which is below the tree. Become one is called, another Becoming - they advise from staves - and Shall-be is third. Wise laws they had, of life they murmured from cuttings of wood. Swelling is the tree's bark, the strands of fate for men.*

Urd is existence, the exhalation-manifestation of existence. First of the three she is the weaver of all their energies. She is a goad that prompts birth, life, death, and birth. Her energy is material control and domination over the fortifications of the inner and outer bodymind. Urd is a pulsating sexual energy that vivifies all that lives, a prodigious throbbing that is everywhere, in everything, a cosmic wave that ripples in human form. Urd is action and back-action, motion and backward motion, deed and back-deed.

Verdandi is structure, the maternal waters that solidify to form biological complexity. Second of the three she is terrestrial space, the external, natural, and rational organization of awareness, of all that lives. She is the seething ooze from which life stirs the bloody boiling waters of firmament, primal matter. Her energy is sustaining and preserving, poised between Urd and Skuld she represents the lower and upper waters of the Well, respectfully, or that which is already formed and created, and the potential of what is still possible. As mediator she can reverse thought or revert to a previous condition or manner of being. Verdandi makes clear the energy of time and space.

Skuld is potential, the all in all, the nothing in nothing, that which creates but is not created, that which exists without existence, meaning, the primal substance that forever bubbles and seethes. Beyond past and purpose, beyond time and space, she is multiversal energy personified, a sacred mystery never fully understood. She alone is the home of spirit, or the energy to be nothing, able to be anything, which is the primordial source of all life. As this primary element she molds and sways, chips and chisels form without form, compressing and concentrating human freedom. Skuld is the sky that opens above when viewed within the sacred grove, a penetration from heaven to earth, a lightening strike that shreds the fabric of matter, the rupture of inert static states, or waves that undulate beneath the surface of all things. More then this power she is over-power, the urge to be victorious in sacrifice, or primordial creation and so only proportional to that offered. Skuld is entangled order, intimate connectivity.

Urd and Verdandi *advise from staves*, create and give council through runes. The word rúna indicates an "intimate (female) friend", and rúnar is "secret, hidden lore, wisdom", sometimes the 'mysteries of giants', but always (physically) written characters or those symbols that are 'cut on a stick'. This may further indicate that caring women, for the benefit of humans, gave runes. Since Ask and Embla were given human form, differentiating them from tree form, the verse: *swelling is the tree's bark, the strands of fate for men*, would indicate that runes are written on human skin by Urd and Verdandi. Just as runes are carved on wood, the Norns etch Urlag upon humans. Markings made on not just the body's largest organ but on the 'sheath' of birth and rebirth, upon DNA itself; and though the strophe relates that only two of these maidens advise humans, all three offer *wise laws* and *murmur* (speak, council, enchant) from *cuttings of wood* (human bodymind).

These three, Urd, Verdandi, and Skuld, represent - like Óð, Hoenir, and Lodur - aspects of human body, mind, and soul. And like a new yew that grows within the hollow trunk of an old yew, so too does our new life animate past dimension. Just as Lif and Lifthrasir will live within the World Tree - sustained from its sap, surviving the end-time - for they are the life pulse of the new Tree upon a new earth.

Regarding Óð's 'breath of life', Urd is an exhale (existence), Verdandi an inhale (structure), and Skuld the pause between breaths (potential). From this natural retention Skuld releases into Urd who then becomes the exhale that prompts Veranda's inhale or structured creation, which draws 'in' to being.

Finally, regarding predestination - for those who seek seiðr wisdom - at no time does an outcome for time, space, or matter exist. Within all things - including being, the soul - at every moment there exist infinite probabilities or forever change. With change comes new courses of action, and with new courses of action comes new direction of possible outcomes.

~ ~ ~

Völuspá - The Great War

Vol.21: *I remember the folk-battle, the first in the realm, where Gold-draught they supported on an anvil's point, yoking her in the High Hall, with their hands burning her. Three times burned - three times! - three times born again, still she lives on.*

I remember the folk-battle, the first in the realm. War is the movement from disorder to order, an attempt to return unity to multiplicity. All wars have opposing forces, the 'good-guys' and 'bad-guys' for example, but to categorize either the Ensi or Wana into one of these categories would detract from the heart at hand. Whether or not there are missing strophes here, 'jumping' it seems from a creation tale to a war story, is of little concern to this commentary. Primarily the focus is on understanding seiðr-nature, which leads in this circumstance to what is known of the Ensi and Wana. Clearly there is far more information on the former than the latter, far more clarity regarding Ensic energy than Wanic energy. Broadly:

- The Ensi are war gods who represent: solidity-regeneration-certain form. Monoversal energy and the realm of stability; the sum of limited expanse; creation; settled and 'civilized' energy; the known; physical; the walls of Ensigart; etc.

- The Wana are fertility gods who represent: fluidity-rejuvenation-imaginative force. Multiversal energy and the stuff of dreams; the sum of all probabilities; chaos; primal and wild, often Jotunic energy; the unknown; psychic; wide-open spaces; etc.

Additionally, there are several other points regarding the Wana that will be examined here, namely: the practice of incest, their kinship to Alfar-Elves, and their relationship with Finno-Ugric shamanism.

- Incest. The definition of incest varies from one culture to another, meaning the definition may be interpreted according to place. For example, a brother and sister marriage could refer to half-brother and half-sister. Or, 'brother' could refer to any male relation: grandfather, father, uncle, cousin, and the same for 'sister' being any female relation. Perhaps the 'royal' line here - assuming the Wana recognized such a notion - ran through the female bloodline, if so, a man would need to marry any female relation to maintain sovereignty. Whatever the case may be, a sibling marriage assuredly represents a wedding of equality. Meaning, that Njord and Nerthus, or Frey and Freyja stood as equals, unlike the Ensic model where relationships appear more male-dominated.

- Alfar-Elves. Regarding any Wanic kinship to Alfar - the latter being god-entities of nature, fertility, and animistic beliefs - Snorri often considered these two groups synonymous, which has perhaps contributed to the current notion of the Wana having evolved into the Huldre, which is simply the exchange of one obscure idea for another.

Intuitively, the Wana and Alfar are separate energy entities, the latter having the ability to change shape at will, and are denizens of art and artistry. Because they are involved with fertility energy they are often confused with the Wana; however, seiðr-wise, Alfar more closely resemble the náttúrur as mentioned in *Eiríks saga rauða*.

A mature seiðus' companion entities can be any number of wights - ancestral, plant, or animal - but the best is that of a non-corporeal seiðu. In Finnish shamanism, for example, a shaman's soul - or tietäjä, meaning "wise man, healing man, sorcerer" - maintains its capacity to shamanize (to include healing), and can choose to assist in the workings of other shamans. This then, too, can be the 'power' behind a náttúrur or 'nature spirit'. If so, and as Davidson suggests, then Alfar could respond as companion entities to qualified seiðus; perhaps even representing enlightened or ascended beings. (1)

- Finno-Ugric shamanism. There exist several references in the Lore mentioning Sámi, 'Lapp', or Finnish magic-users, undoubtedly the indigenous circumpolar shamans of Northern Europe. (2)   Likewise, there is no doubt that circumpolar shamanism played a role in the accessing of seiðr - and possibly the other aspects of soulcrafting - the question is: "To what extent?"

As has already been stated, there exist two complete systems - Wanic esoterica and Sámi-Finnish shamanism - that mutually and agreeably exchanged information-techniques between themselves that may have resulted in the definition-refinement of something quite unique to Heathenry, namely: seiðr, the penetration of consciousness to access the flow of Wyrd, or trance. In appearance, the Ensic model is more religious whereas the Wanic-Sámi model is more nature-animism spirituality.

Intuitively, the Wana are and project:

- A nomadic tribe who excel at horsemanship and warfare; revere female warriors known as 'valkryies'; and view the northlands as a place of violent wind-Jotuns;

- They prize gold above all other metals, believing it to be a gift from their 'gods', and are excellent gold craftsmen; venerate the plough for its fertility, the yoke for its union and discipline, the sword for its eternal synthesis (perhaps representing even the wedding of siblings), and the flask as a symbol of preservation and gifting.

- They honor a sky father and water mother; sacrifice criminals and strangers by beheading or burning them in sacred fire; and the cave in which Loki was bound resides on a mountain in Wanaheim.

- Have the ability to take on any form, including Jotunic; are magic-users, or crafters of mægen; the most holy among them has the ability to shed tears of gold; they make annual sacrifices of beautiful gold objects in deep mountain lakes; teach the use of cannabis to induce trance; have no writing system, saving the use of sigils for more spiritual ends (which includes tattoos as sacred body art).

- Their great embrace, exuberance, and seeming ease towards all of life - both joy and turmoil - compels their envious enemies to consider them 'bestial' and practitioners of 'incest'; believe in life-after-death so bury their dead with rich objects for the next life (to enjoy upon their return); seem to ever seek out and secure peace for the promotion of fertility and the continuation of life on earth.

- Possess great power-objects - like girdles of strength, bows of perfect aim, and ships that can change shape; venerate great trees and hold council meetings in sacred groves.

- Possess incredible animals - like three-headed dogs and gigantic serpents; view the wolf as a dark opponent of their 'earth powers'; especially honor the deer, goat, and eagle, while viewing the horse as a noble beast of both war and death.

Factually (but rendered collectively below), the Sámi-Finnish shaman ("noaide"):
- Is part of a nomadic tribe who are historically reindeer herders.

- Has an animistic worldview where spiritual content is more important than earth-bound ethics; gods and other entities live in the three realms of 'Heaven' (above, gods), 'Earth' (middle, humans and animals), and 'Underworld' (below, the dead); Sun, Moon, Thunder, Hunt(ing), and Wind are gods; all god-forms have both 'good' and 'evil' traits; the sun and solar energy are feminine; men primarily honor the gods while women primarily honor the goddesses;

- Is a spiritual leader who interprets the will of the gods and supernatural phenomena for the benefit of their siida (akin to 'sippe'?) or village; noaides are individuals who have mastered the soul and so immune to illness and - to a degree - death; noaides go on soul-journeys to the realm of death, or *sàivu*; noaides are healers who perform sacrifices to assure a balance between humans and gods, who communicate with animals to secure a successful hunt, and whose well-developed soul-immunity is used to bolster the community; noaides work with spirits who assist them in their endeavors; noaides work as spiritual guides and councilors - either in groups or singly - to intervene in conflicts, unveil the past and predict the future, perform social work, work as healer-doctor, find lost objects, and act as story-teller; noaides use joik, or singing-chanting, 'on' someone or something; the most important tool of a noaide is their drum.

Clearly, a composite of these elements - Wanic and Finno-Ugric shamanism - creates a picture of both similarities and differences that could easily define the unique worldview and skill traits commonly found in a seiðr practitioner.

Chief among the Ensi is Odin, as to who this may be for the Wana is unsure. Some accounts acknowledge Njord as their leader, who, after the war - along with his children Frey and Freyja - is given as hostage in exchange for Hoenir and Mimir. A trade the Wana came to determine as being unfair. Another possiblity for cheiftain could be Gullveig. From this narrative she appears to be the first Wana to encounter the Ensi. At the very least her role would be that of emissary. The ill-treatment she received would certainly explain the hostility and subsequent First Great War.

Regarding Njord, little is known of him, even less of his name, which could mean everything from 'sponge' and 'charmed; good luck', to 'spy; scouting; look out' and 'strait'. It is known that during samal and oath-taking his name was called along with Frey and Odin (sometimes Thor); and some kennings for Njord are: 'Scion of the Wana', the 'Wana God', and 'God Without Blemish'. (3) Of note, regarding a 'scion', this is a length of stem taken from a plant and grafted onto the rootstock of another plant, which could imply he was fully adopted into the Ensi tribe. Likewise, it also means an heir or descendent, so Njord's name could mean "Descendent of the Wana".

Tactitus includes a female deity here: Nerthus, and Davidson links the two - Njord and Nerthus - as possible parents to Frey and Freyja. Energy-wise they, like their offspring, are twins: Njord having the impression of a great expanse or huge circumference, and Nerthus of a companion, friend, and matron. Further, psychically, a tendril connects them with Ægir and Ran, perhaps as their parents, grandparents to Frey and Freyja.

Njord-Nerthus, as divine twins and co-cheiftains of the Wana would represent primal force, birth, and procreation - a classic example of fecundity. Twins, as symbols of totality, represent the best of both worlds, or an integration of opposites. As gods of fluidity they would represent the lower-ocean and the upper-ocean, or lower- and upper-consciousness; or, both the source of life and the tide that ever returns or folds back unto itself. By way of water they could be related to Ægir-Ran, the primordial ocean (deeply profound consciousness), if so it could be concluded that their birth was prompted from Ginnunga-gap itself, or perhaps they are one of the off-springs of Hvergelmir.

Gullveig as a possible emissary, the custodian of Wanic ideals, represents the golden flask that contains a "golden draught". She is a sip of something precious: of spiritual preservation and gifting. Perhaps, she is an essence the Ensi are not familiar with at this stage of their experience. Gold is easily related to the sun and solar light, or divine intelligence. The sun in man would be the human heart, so too would gold be the heart of earth. Following the idea of Nornic gifts, perhaps Gullveig was a bounty the Ensi could not match: supreme spiritual gifts. Anyroad, with her three rebirths, she personifies - and so offers - spiritual determination. At the least, to those who seek seiðr initiation, she is a volatile formula for transitory and dissembling energy.

Three times burned - three times! - three times born again, yet she lives on. Gullveig is a singular trinity. Alone, she is positive, negative, and neutral; she is sub-conscious, conscious, and supra-conscious, she is a teacher of seiðr, a master teacher, and an ascended master able to relate the knowledge of all time, space, and matter. Hers was a shamanic death, the destruction of her external identity and existence making way for the revelation of inner being.   She is an inspiration to all seiðus, a compassionate guide and protectress from all harm.

Being burnt and resurrected three times, then being renamed-rebirthed as Heið, would reassemble her as the purest and truest expression of primal and multiversal attainment, or a supreme being. In short, this seiðr scholar proposes that Gullveig's transformation into Heið created nothing less then the swastika (Sanskrit: "auspicious"). Akin to the four dwarves who 'support' the world's four corners, guardians of the threshold of consciousness, Gullveig in her fourth incarnation became a warder of order, the symbol of spatiality. (4)   First she was Gullveig - organic material existence, the 'heart of earth', supreme illumination, a golden elixer of intelligence and action; then she was killed, burnt and reborn as strength and movement. The second death she was reborn as deliverance and forebearance; concentrated yet infinite, something still without form or firmness so they killed her and burnt her again. After the third death and burning she emerged as light without limit, as Heið the Clear and Brilliant, or the clear light of intuitive knowledge and truth. Each forging upon the Ensic anvil made her stronger than before, overcoming intense external suffering and loss, becoming detached of her old form, she embraced her new focus: spiritual enlightenment.   Each forging representing an 'arm', an extention of her inner clairity; symbolically depicted as the sunwheel. Simply, she is the cardinal points and the four seasons, the succession of generations and the four stages of life; deeply, she is the refined essence of all that is.

As representative of the Wana, Gullveig came as nothingness, the physical manifestation of Ginnunga-gap, or the seething absolute. As such she was incomprehensible to the form-embracing Ensi, which filled their hearts with fear of the unknown and unknowable. As war-gods, as leaders of all things physical, she stood in their Hall, an affront to all organization and stability, all surety and tangibility. Destroying her brought another form: Heið, the "clear" and "brilliant", a reflection of the conversion from physical to spiritual, from weakness to strength, from mortal to immortal.

Exclusively:
> *Heið she is called when she arrives at built houses,*
> *choosing well to seethe, to foretell, all sense-consciousness –*
> *marking and riding her staff.*
> *To chant with knowing, to bring ease and comfort through mindful*
> *enchanting; ever washing the head with sweet and fragrant odor,*
> *there to rid ill-brewings.*

Being reborn, the first phoenix rising from flames, she is periodic and needful regeneration. As Gullveig-Heið she leads by example, gifting us with the wisdom to live fully in every moment, to flow and change and overcome difficulty to emerge resplendent and triumphant, and in so doing, embrace life in its fullest clarity. This mystic transformation, the renewal of multiversal existence, creates so much consternation that she enrages the Ensi against her. (5) Yet she stands, as her name and actions attest, as the embodiment of indestructible supreme virtue, a reflection of elevated and pure qualities, or the volatile, transitory, and dissembling energy of seiðr.

Several accounts exist in the Lore relating the Ensi's distrust of seiðr. If Gullveig is latent primal matter then her death and burning herald the end of profanity, of the uninitiated and unworthy aspect of being. Easy to see then how she came to represent, to the Ensi, a symbol of all things dark and deadly, unknown and so fearful. For the Wana and those who study their innermost coursings - the accessors of seiðr - she is a call to actively engage in the 'death' of all that is inferior within, so that only forged strength and clarity remains.

Gullveig-Heið is the luminous woman, exclusively: She Who Accounts for the Length of Life, or Goddess of Destiny. Her brilliance is more luminous then golden, more sunshine then goldshine. This signifies her inner radiance - the golden draught, the fiery deluge - that all living beings drink.

Exiled from, but not so easily cast-off, as her multiple deaths and rebirths attest, she demonstrated her violent whirlwind ability by traveling from the Ensi innangart to Midworld. There she quickly became known for the accuracy of her predictions - especially during sacrificial tides - and as a goddess of death and regeneration. For every time she died, she journeyed to Hella's Hall, only to return again. To honor her, surround an icon of her with a mound of golden coins. The stag, an ancient symbol of the multiverse, related to the Tree of Life, is sacred to her. As an emblem of regeneration and growth, gnawing on the leaves of the World Tree but remaining unharmed - unlike other animals that die from the experience - the stag, like the serpent, is related to heaven and earth (the serpent specifically to earth and underworld). Seiðr-wise, the stag is a beast of journey to the otherworlds, or a teacher of psychic projection.

The stag is a wondrous animal, its speed, agility, and grace have the ability to be imparted as gifts; their energy is both cosmic and solar, an all encompassing and invigorating life-force. Their horns represent that-which-is-above, particularly when worn on the head; and they are thought to carry the Pole Star between their eyes and the moon in their heart. (6) In world myth it is the messenger of a kind and caring goddess, often depicted as its mother.

Exclusively Gullveig-Heið, 'golden-brilliance', is Earth Mother, Gold Mother, and it was perhaps her radiant sexuality that Odin found distasteful, in that he could not control her. Odin is often depicted subduing females - perhaps even seeking to usurp their contributions to birth and birthing - which can only confuse and detract from the valuable skills he can impart. Suggestively, after the three Jotun maidens gave their gifts, like the cast-off and uninvited 'fairy godmothers' of myth, Gullveig came to remind Odin of his familial obligations. By sending Heimdallr to teach humans - advising him to instruct them in their earthly roles, to gift them with runes - Odin promoted Heimdallr as world-mediator, as world-surveyor. Speculatively, perhaps Gullveig pointed out that this was an inappropriate choice for a would-be father figure to play, not having direct contact with his own offspring; and as can be assumed, Odin does not take well to either having his decisions questioned or being admonishment. Along similar lines, the tale of Odin and Brunhild indicates another defunct relationship.

Gullveig-Heið appears then to stand in contrast to Odin and his often one-minded Ragnarök focus. (reference 5) She appears to offer immediate direction, providing instruction and enabling entrance into all realms of existence, allowing direct communication with her instead of an intermediary. She is a living example of the ability to access, in rapid succession no less, the lower-dead and higher-living worlds of rejuvenation and spiritual potential. Odin, as All-Father, teaches either indirectly or through Heimdallr such useful skills as poetry and music, weaponry and warfare, but is not always forthcoming with his knowledge. Conversely, Gullveig-Heid - as goddess of celestial fire and infinite bounty, as healer and provider, as fecund life giver - appears to nurture the seiðu as All-Mother of mystic might and mægen.

References
(1) Davidson. Reference: *Road to Hel*; H.R.E. Davidson; New York, 1968; pages 111-115.

(2) Sámi-Finnish magic users. Reference: *Egil's saga, Haraldar saga hárfagra, Heimskringla, Historia Norwegica, Njáls saga*, and *Vatndaela saga*, for example.

(3) God Without Blemish. Reference: *Norse Mythology - Legends of Gods and Heroes*; P.A. Munch; 1942; page 13.

(4) Threshold of consciousness. *Psychology of Alchemy*; C. Jung; 1953; throughout.

(5) She enrages the Ensi against her. In this early example, the Ensi - as war gods or entities of physical existence - feared her otherworldliness. This changed however when Odin himself hung on the tree.

(6) The Pole Star between their eyes. As still seen today in modern Europe: the stag with a cross upon its brow.

~ ~ ~

Vol.22: *Heið she is called when she arrives at built houses, choosing well to seethe, to foretell, all sense-consciousness - marking and riding her staff. To chant with knowing, to bring ease and comfort through mindful enchanting; ever washing the head with sweet and fragrant odor, there to rid ill-brewings.*

..when she arrives at built houses. There are several places to do seiðr: in houses, in wild places, on burial mounds, etc. Suggestively, those who seek to be seiðus should be "homeless and wandering shamans", meaning free to travel where called or needed. (1) From the accounts of völvas in the Lore, this could have been the case, perhaps even an aspect of Heathen culture and tradition. Nor, seemingly, should seiðus commit to a singular sippe or tribe, their focus apparently too large for such structures - the nature of seiðr being that of All over a few. It appears historically that seiðus congregated at designated learning centers, colleges of spiritual learning and focus. (2)

Exclusively but energetically it is best for master seiðus to abstain from the commitment and ties of society - emotionally and socially - to focus predominantly on living and maintaining a permanent condition of seiðr. Long-lasting relationships with sippe-kindred's, though warm and inviting at times, can detract-distract from the absolute focus needed for inner spiritual work, for communion with Wyrd consciousness. But then, it may simply be a matter of which-comes-first. Many seiðus who fully devote their lives to this course develop a natural disinterest in external relationships, often recognizing and so responding fully to fundamental-cellular change that occurs through this Wyrd work.

This may further explain the difficulty some seiðus encounter when committed to a personal relationship. The energy it takes to maintain this form of association diminishes the focus of thought, word, and deed necessary for full commitment to Folksoul. Ginnunga-gapic energy is stored in every cell of being; even so, only through inner and outer seiðr focus can it be brought forth into Midworld for the benefit of Folksoul.

Seiðus should, where able, direct their attention solely on study and application of study, on acquiring knowledge and the application of that knowledge. Living alone is ideal, for in doing so the seiðu is left with only the Tivar and Vettir, and in so doing realize great benefit sooner. Advantage that, in turn, can be - must be - shared with sippes and tribes.

Seiðus outwardly honor their Tivar and Vettir while inwardly working on embodying the vast truth of all wights, a dedicated focus that should be carried out for no less then twelve (12) years. Seiðus must understand the nature of reality before being able to manipulate it well. Physical reality, which Gullveig-Heið burned away, teaches that control is necessary to create-mold reality. After all, it is not about outward senses but inner ones.

Progressing to the next level, concentration should be upon knowledge gained; and if there exists any doubt regarding the self-creation of reality, then the practitioner becomes 'stuck' at a lower level. Consciousness must be manipulated at the level above physical density so that the formation of images and thoughts, before they reach physical form, can be controlled and manipulated for the benefit of others. From this platform does the seiðu continual expand their horizon.

After twelve years a seiðu should earn and so acquire a staff as symbol of their dedication and role within the tribes. They may also have runes or staves as tools of inner awareness. Seiðus should honor the hours of day and night with blot and faining, depending on their level of commitment. The Between times are best: dawn, noon, dusk, and midnight, for there is great wisdom to be had by recognizing and participating with the forces during these points of coordination.

Seiðus should first offer earth, then water, and finally breathe in all they do. Any seiðu who has been practicing for even a short period of time can relate how quickly they loose health and vitality, intuition and connectedness, when they allow themselves to slip into the routines of regular souls. There is potency and competence, vast understanding and tremendous energy to be had from self-discipline and dedication, mostly by way of maintaining Tivarity, so to speak. In short, wisdom comes only with dedication.

For seiðus who use herbs to enhance consciousness, it is wise to refrain from recreational use of such aids. Use them exclusively for spiritual purposes and only within sacred and controlled space.

Seiðus are healthy souls because seiðr generates health. If you are practicing seiðr and are ill or prone to sickness, stressful or anxious, feel irritable and unbalanced, restless or lack sleep, poor or have insufficient funds, and become angry or explode over trifling things, you are doing something wrong. True seiðr brings strength to bodymind and soul, it brings material wealth and psychic surety, it brings willpower and exaltation; it brings discernment and discrimination; it is the distaff on which the twin threads of happiness and ecstasy are wound. The most dedicated of seiðus will refrain from regular sexual relations, knowing that the body's sap, once depleted, takes time to replenish itself. Holding onto this life-source, they journey unhindered and unmolested in all realms. This gold essence, this dew upon the World Tree, upholds a seiðus' life. Dew is the draught of spiritual illumination - a true alu of seiðr - the drinking of which shines through the eyes and reddens the cheeks. It is no less then the quintessence of blood.

Above all else, it is more about mental discipline than physical discipline; do one and the other will follow.

..ever washing the head with sweet and fragrant odor, there to rid ill-brewings. Admittedly, this verse commentary is based on lay-linguistics. As a seiðr scholar with over thirty-five years of hands-on occult training and involvement - and that this work is focused primarily on mystic awareness - there will be heavy emphasis on energy-intuition over exact translation. Therefore, after inner reflection and otherworldly guidance, this verse has been rendered transcendentally.

References
(1) "Homeless and wandering shamans". A direct quote from Freya Aswynn (equally as the sentiment of this seiðr scholar).

(2) Colleges of spiritual learning. Reference: *Haralds saga hárfagra*, and *Heimskringla*.

~ ~ ~

Vol.23: *Then went the ruling powers [the decision makers] to their tranquil and proud stools [the seats of decision-making]; the holy gods gathering in council. Whether the Ensi are bound-obliged to pay tribute, or are the gods bound-obliged to share brotherhood?*

It would appear the Ensi did not consider killing a guest in their Hall as an offense - not in the least objectionable - and it seems that compensating the Wana would include accepting them as kin; perhaps to do so would include recognizing the Wana as having equal status. Imaginably the Wana could have demanded equality as a form of compensation. Then again, since Gullveig was killed, burnt, and reborn, three times - to emerge unscathed as Heið - is that considered murder?

According to *Gragas*, if this could be considered applicable, there must be "mortal-wound witnesses". (1) Now, there were certainly witnesses to mortal wounds, and the subsequent burnings that came with them, but again, nothing that resulted in permanent death. Regarding *brotherhood*, in that Gullveig-Heið lived - personally able to speak as witness to her own murder - a truce needed to be discussed; depending of course on whether the Ensi were willing to truce. If they were, this temporary cessation to hostilities would have assured that the "..earth upholds the truce, on high the sky bounds it, and around it is the red ocean which encompasses all lands we have knowledge of." (2) Anyroad, it is clear the Ensi chose another course of action.

References
(1) Mortal-wound witnesses. Reference: *The Codex Regius of Gragas*, section 87, Treatment of Homicide.

(2) We have knowledge of. Reference: *The Codex Regius of Gragas*, section 114, Truce Speech.

~ ~ ~

Vol.24: *Odin hurled [a spear] over a corner of heaven, over the folk - that was the folk-battle, first ever where they lived. Broken then were the wooden walls, the boards of Ensigart; with prowess the Wana made themselves unharmed by spear, fighting unharmed, treading on [Ensi] ground.*

Odin hurled [a spear] over a corner of heaven, over the folk. This is widely considered a form of warrior magic, or that by casting a spear over the enemy a warrior 'claims' their lives as his own. Spears are symbols of royalty and of earth, which signifies solidity and wealth. Clearly however, Odin's spell casting is not strong enough to repel Wanic strength.

Broken then were the wooden walls, the boards of Ensigart; with prowess the Wana made themselves unharmed by spear, fighting unharmed, treading on [Ensi] ground. It appears the Wana used magic to both remove themselves from overall harm and from the spell cast by Odin. Regardless, whether by war-skill and force of arm or of enchantment the Wana stand as victors; vindicated in the unwarranted ill-treatment of Gullveig-Heið, exalted through action, for all warfare presupposes affinity until the victor stands over the vanquished. Especially in this circumstance, magical battles are more then strength of arms but of spiritual worth, and here, the Wana stand rightly recognized.

~ ~ ~

[Interpolated] *Upon the Great Ones came the responsibility for frith; kinship to assure accord in all worlds. The blessing songs of Grotti rang loud and pure with pleasing sound. Into this air did the Great Ones - Jotun, Ensi, and Wana alike - exchange hostages.*

A wondrous frith prevailed in all the worlds; a compact between Jotuns, Ensi, and Wana was created to ease all discordant resonance. From the Wana came Njord, the twins Frey and Freyja, and Kvasir to live among the Ensi. The Ensi sent Hoenir, and the Jotuns send Mimir, both to live among the Wana.

~ ~ ~

[Interpolated] *Then came blowing wind, hissing like a serpent, Blast offering to rebuild the great Ensigart walls. From Midnight Sun to Burning Wheel did he toil with proud steed Svadilfari, seeking sun and moon and Freyja as payment. Trickery his only reward, bloodshed on Ensigart's ground.*

Blast is the Jotun's name who rebuilt the walls of Ensigart, he is listed as a rimthursar or being who emerged from primordial ice. Such Jotuns, beings of supreme cold, represent transition from consciousness to unconsciousness, or resistance to all things superior. After the Great War he offered to rebuild Ensigart's walls - apparently a task the Ensi could not do alone - in exchange for Sunna, Mani, and Freyja, or the sun, moon, and stars.

Freyja, aside from her close ties to seiðr, is intimately linked with amber, which is an Indo-European word for 'sky' and has the ability to strengthen a seiðu's energy connection to the stars. Outwardly amber is symbolic of protection, having the ability to absorb negativity, perhaps even 'sending' a warning of impeding harm, in which case, it would be associated with Luck. Seiðr-wise amber has the energy of 'mother earth' and protective-supportive energy.

If the amber here is a necklace it represents cosmic and erotic sex, as a girdle it reflects moral virtue. If Freyja indeed had sex with four dwarves for her amber necklace this would signify her ability to conquer, through sex, terrestrial space, or human ignorance. Assuredly, this would lead to the attainment of true wisdom, and intuitively, this would explain her ability to shed tears of gold or amber, a sign of holiness to ancient Heathenry. Sun, moon, and sky, combined, would then represent conscious wisdom, deep-wisdom, and spirit - a mighty price indeed.

Trickery his only reward, bloodshed on Ensigart's ground. As will be seen in the next strophe.

~ ~ ~

Vol.25: *Then went the ruling powers [the decision makers] to their tranquil and proud stools [the seats of decision-making]; the holy gods gathering in council. Who lifted into the air a crafty mix of discord, whether to release to the Jotun's quarter [their direction, area] the divine inheritance, the maiden of good conduct.*

Who lifted into the air a crafty mix of discord. Air is more then a means of communication but creativity itself. It is wind and speech, movement and emergence, and in this case it has become contaminated with strife.

..whether to release to the Jotun's quarter [their direction, area] the divine inheritance, the maiden of good conduct. Releasing to the Jotun's quarter would be sending the sun (conscious wisdom), moon (deep-wisdom), and Freyja-stars (spirit) to Jotunheim. Considering what Jotun's represent and what a combination of the Sunna, Mani, and Freyja represent, this would certainly be catastrophic for the Ensi. The divine inheritance here is Sunna and Mani, and the maiden of good conduct is Freyja.

~ ~ ~

Vol.26: *Thor alone was troubled then, stifling his wrath, he seldom sits still when hearing such things. Violated and dead are the oaths, words sworn to - speech having lost its strength, the middle ground torn asunder.*

Thor alone was troubled then, stifling his wrath, he seldom sits still when hearing such things. For the second time, an Ensi breaks the bonds of hospitality, in this case specifically, of an oath given.

Violated and dead are the oaths, words sworn to - speech having lost its strength, the middle ground torn asunder. Clearly, when lies are spoken oaths - all words - have no meaning. The 'middle ground' here was the oath-ground, or the coming together of two groups, as seen in the previous strophe - *Who lifted into the air a crafty mix of discord,* the 'mix' here being an accord struck between the Ensi and Jotuns. Little wonder then that the Ensi are ill respected amongst Jotuns, the oldest and often wisest denizens of all worlds.

~ ~ ~

Vol.27 [Interpolated]: *On Midworld this is why you sent the World Brightener Odin, why you sent the white Wanic fire, the bringer of nine virtues. Blessed Father Heimdallr, the fire-auger, teacher of the human soul, son of nine mothers; he alone could do what you - Warlord - could not. Reconciliation you sought and treaty too Odin, but no friend to accord have you ever been.*

In this interpolated strophe an attempt is made to both create a flow within the text, affording an independent sequence, and to briefly mention events to the more familiar reader. The inference here is: after several failed attempts to reconcile the mutually supportive groups - Jotuns, Ensi, and Wana - Odin must send an individual to speak on his behalf, someone respected by all parties concerned. That individual is Heimdallr.

Up to this point, according to Völuspá: Odin and his brothers killed Aurgelmir; then (presumably) Odin, or all three of them, sought to exclude the Jotuns from human creation (denying his own lineage); then Odin murdered Gullveig three times; and instead of admitting the breaking of frith he started the Great War. Following this, Thor, Odin's son, kills a Jotun, breaking an oath. War-Father's reputation for being ambiguous at best, volatile and untrustworthy at least, appears as well deserved as it is clearly laid out in the Lore; which is why it would behoove him to have an emissary represent his good intent, even as he fails to express this himself.

Emissaries are representatives of the higher purpose and goals of an individual or government. It is honor-worthy to be chosen as an emissary in that such individuals represent the highest and best virtues; therefore, emissaries are - or should be - outstanding facilitators or interpreters of good will. Contrary to Loki's mocking from *Lokasenna* 48: "Be silent Heimdallr! In days long gone was a dark task fixed to you; with stiff back you ever stand, Warder of heaven, ever watching". Being sent out from a familiar homeland to reside in an unfamiliar one for an extended period of time, having no authority over this new land, acting as a messenger or spokesman, and in this circumstance, something of a prophet, Heimdallr was afforded a great honor - appointed by Odin to declare his will over all humans, to be chief mediator or intermediary.

Nor is this an alien concept. Akin to the exchange of hostages emissaries have a long history even among the Indo-Europeans. Odin - as claimant to the rulership of Midworld and humans - seems to have become detached from both of these through his deeds, so he chose the one entity who surveys all the worlds, whose hearing is so acute that he can hear the growth of both wool and grass. Heimdallr is the divine watchman, ever vigilant, with perfect vision in full sun or dark moon, warder of the rainbow, and possessor of Gjallarhorn. As a heavenly horseman his steed can reach and perhaps exceed the speed of light, projecting his own brilliance before him. Heimdallr's role is to aid humans - to give them point of place and purpose - teaching them how to produce fire, use the healing herbs, to plant fields, and domesticate animals. He teaches them to craft and forge, to use the loom and net, bow and spear. He shows them the building of temples and the honoring of High Ones, sharing with them runes. For these reasons, and many more, he was known as Rig among humans: 'ruler, king'. Rix or rig is Old Irish for "king"; Old High German rihhi, "ruler, powerful, rich"; Old English rice, "wealthy, powerful, mighty"; all from Proto-Indo-European *reg-, "direct, rule; move in a straight line". In short, Heimdallr is All-Friend to all men.

Greatest of all Heimdallr-Rig's gifts were runes: "From the grove came Rig striding, runes he brought to teach them", *Rigsthula* 36. (1) Here again is the emissarial role explored: Odin took the runes for himself while suspended on the World Tree - as an individual act - Heimdallr brought them to Midworld for the benefit of all humans (the human soul). As to exactly what these runes may be or whether they were the same as taught to him by his nine mothers or ones given to him by Odin to share - or a combination of both - is uncertain.

From inner perception, the nine runes are stepping stones upon the spiritual path, each a progression of the other, like rungs on a ladder, best taken one at a time. Exclusively, the nine runes given by Heimdallr to humans are (with emphasis for seiðus):

The Thrall, or Body Runes
Hearer, Listener. The *Rune of Hearing*, practicing, and proclaiming what has been heard. Listening requires concentration, it requires setting aside inner thoughts to focus on new information, or the ability to liberate preconceived notions (dogma) for the attainment of inner wisdom.

Self-Reliant, Self-Responsible. The *Rune of Self-Reliance*, self-rule, self-sufficiency, and self-determination. Being self-reliant requires the Rune of Hearing, it necessitates either an acquired or self-taught ability to not just learn something new but to allow it to become part of being (instantly for some, over an extended period for others).

Greater Intelligence, Self-Sacrifise. The *Rune of Greater Intelligence* represents souls who have achieved consciousness on every level of being and chosen to sacrifise their soul for the benefit of the Folksoul. Such souls are filled with integrity. They place Law and Truth above all actions, they do not steal or lie, they are steady in their work (to include seiðr), they never praise themselves or disparage others, and they do not gather great wealth (so are not easily bribed or compelled towards greed). All seiðus should 'own' this rune.

The Karl, or Mind Runes
Action-Reaction, Practical Consciousness. The *Rune of Practical Consciousness* is a condition of neutrality. First, consciousness is a condition of awareness, therefore, simply being awake - having a job, responsible for a family, for example - does not automatically imply consciousness. From an energy perspective this rune aids the seiðu to both be rid of and work through-around the energies of greed, hate, and delusion-fantasy. Beyond the dynamic of action-reaction this rune's energy is one of conscious response.

Twin, Self-Same. The *Rune of Self-Same*, or the Twin Rune, for its fluctuating energy of mortal and immortal. Meaning, at this point, the soul can either progress towards the Above Worlds or to the Lower Worlds, towards light or darkness. This rune is an oath to pursue or not pursue virtue, specifically: to kill or to let live, to be truthful or to lie, to create or to steal, to have sex or not, to be sober or drunk.

Concord, Merging. The *Rune of Concord* is the energy of intergration integrity at the cellular level. For seiðus this means to no longer distinguish between what is inside of them and what is outside of them. This is the supreme ability to learn from not just personal experience but every experience, of personal experience over book-learning, of viewpoint over conduct. This rune's energy is a realization of the natural state of being, of stability, and of longevity.

The Jarl, or Soul Runes
Völva, Vitki, Magic. The *Rune of Wisdom* belongs to those who have ascended skill in seiðr to become a mystic, a skald, a lawspeaker, a healer. Beyond body, beyond mind, this energy is unfailing all-accomplishment, the embodiment of wisdom; here there is nothing divided. Once attained, the seiðu becomes surrounded and supported by mægen in that all threads of existence course through their being. Safety and calm, blessing and balance are the nature of this rune.

Speaker, Giver. The *Rune of Speaking* is the ability to give proof of experience, to not just teach others but to lay before them - through the evidence of self-control - the mægen available for those who stay steady on this course. It is one thing to hear an experience, another to understand or take it 'in'. This is inner knowledge over external learning, this is completion rather then working-developing. The Rune of Speaking is accustomed insight into the nature of all that lives.

Natural, True Nature. The *Rune of True Nature* is abounding virtue, the supreme integrity, the inner core of all that lives, the primordial essence of all beings, there is nothing beyond this - which is pure, complete, and total awareness. True Nature is extraordinary, the definitive of all mystic secrets, the essentia of Ginnunga-gap. Natural existence is with us from the beginning. Sculpted from Ask and Embla - two seeds that grew into trees, offshoots of the World Tree - humans are already the element by which all things exist or are knowable in any capacity. In this rune is the connecting thread between primal essence and physical essence, which is revealed in the nature of primal essence to divide itself into nine categories, or worlds. This is the fount of life, of all vitality. Natural and True Nature is the peak of Nine Worlds as seen from a single point; no longer shattered or obscured or struggling, but re-formed so that the seiðu lives in the Realm of Spontaneity, the Realm of Presence.

Reference
(1) Rigsthula 36. Also see strophes 44 and 46. Rig's Thule is, literally, 'The Wise-Man Rig', or The Sayings of the Wise-man Rig.

~ ~ ~

Vol.31. *While on High I saw the Valkyries, through my consciousness, arriving from afar. Clearly I remember their horses' weaving ride to the Godfolk. Skuld - duty bound to collect the debt, knowing how to discern knowledge - assuring all have their due, and Bone-Skinner busy at work behind her; [with them are] God-daughter, Battle, Running-Concealment, and Gory-Skinned-Joint. Now has their place been numbered among the Father's Host, set to perform their sacrifice are the Choosers of the Slain, upon the green grassy plain.*

In strophe 27, interpolated, Heimdallr's role in the Age of Accord is clear; to then be followed by Valkyries riding on high - suggestively in response to the next strophe where Baldr's destination is set - indicates the Wolf Age.

While on High I saw the Valkyries, through my consciousness, arriving from afar. Clearly I remember their horses weaving ride to the Godfolk. 'Vit' in the first line means consciousness; Gullveig-Heið is not journeying to this event but observing it from where she is sitting-out. The *horses' weaving ride* indicates these noble animals relationship to burial mounds and burial rites, equally as they are associated with war and the instinctive and deep conscious being. Horses are considered clairvoyant so their appearance here may well foretell Baldr's demise; their ability to weave connects them to the multiverse. (1)

Valkyries are psychopomps - soul chaperons - rudders upon the journey from one realm of existence to another. These shield maidens are fierce clarity and determined luminosity, in seeming contrast to death, which is often seen as darkness and gloom. For learning seiðus, there is great wisdom in this. At all times these Dis - these 'beings of light' - are protective and beatific. They are gloriously gorgeous, outrageously otherworldly, and spiritually sublime. Often depicted wearing feathered cloaks they resemble birds - long-known symbols of the soul - and are renderers of divine aid. Likewise they are messengers, conveying the will of the gods to humans, by extension then they are wise in the ways of trance or communication with the divine. Another task these ladies joyfully carry out is seeing to the needs of great warriors, a role reserved only for pure and virtuous women. Valkyries are symbols of invisible force, descending to Midworld they are like swans from heaven, gracing earth with their presence.

Skuld - duty bound to collect the debt, knowing how to discern knowledge - assuring all have their due. Skuld is a Norn whose role is generally agreed upon as "Shall Be", or "Should", in translation there are other options, as seen above. (Another translation of this line includes a possible role interpreting runes.) As an aspect of what-shall-be, based on deeds-choices made, her role as a Chooser of the Slain makes sense. What more dramatic example then the battlefield is needed to see the immediate results of actions taken?

..[with them are] God-daughter, Battle, Running-Concealment, and Gory-Skinned-Joint. Now has their place been numbered among the Father's Host, set to perform their sacrifice are the Choosers of the Slain, upon the green grassy plain. Valkyrie names are graphic, even in their more subdued translations.

Reference
(1) Multiverse. *Symbols of Transformation*; C. Jung; New York; 1977; throughout.

~ ~ ~

Vol.32: *I see Baldr, blood-smeared god, Odin's child, thread of life fading away. A great beam had grown up, well-shapen, and with a round stick, hoary with age, was laid flat on the ground; greatly praised and decorated, the fair and beautiful mistletoe.*

I see Baldr, blood-smeared god, Odin's child, thread of life fading away. The völva 'sees' Baldr's death both from her mound far away and before his death occurs.

A great beam had grown up, well-shapen, and with a round stick, hoary with age, was laid flat on the ground; greatly praised and decorated, the fair and beautiful mistletoe. This line can be read as both an oak tree and as Baldr (as the 'great beam'), reminiscent perhaps of *The Dream of the Rood*. Oaks become overburdened with mistletoe and may succumb and die, causing them to either fall or be cut down. If this verse implies Baldr then the mistletoe is already an aspect of his being.

There are three ways to examine this myth: natural, based on cyclic seasonal changes; internal, based on transpersonal spirituality; or energy, which is the central focus of this verse commentary. This seiðr scholar then will continue along that thread.

74

It is convenient to categorize Baldr as a sun god, or an entity that is born, suffers death, passes into the realm of death, and is born again; a means that lends itself to comparison with other such entities, like Osirus or Jesus. Or, more credible to the Heathen worldview, this tale can relate the means in which the Tivar withdraw their daily presence and constant interaction from their creation. Now that Heimdallr has shared the nine runes with humans - allowing for Midworld can become independent - they may find their own true and inner nature.

Mistletoe is a hemi- or partial-parasite whose root system draws nutrition from its host tree. Generally, the healing properties and energy properties of oak were associated, incorrectly, to mistletoe for this reason. Found the world over, yet exhibiting many variations - from woody structure to leaf size to poisonous berries to some species having no leaves of their own - these plants can barely be commonly associated one with the other. Just like Baldr cannot be associated with other divine entities that just happen to share a few attributes.

The Icelandic word is mistil + teinn, the former being bird excrement and the latter a twig or stick; so that the word literally means 'dung twig' or 'shit stick'; more romantically referred to as the 'golden bough'. Virgil's *Aeneid* has an interesting account of a golden bough that grows on a special tree in a grove sacred to the Greek Goddess Diana. Her role was much like a Dis of sacred groves and prophecy, of fertility and protection, and to the Between times of dawn and dusk; little wonder mistletoe would grow in her trees being this variety is similar to the European version. Burnt as incense European mistletoe may induce light trance, and carried, it is said to protect the wearer from lightening and snake bites. It is best seen at dawn and dusk when the sun's rays illumine its bright green foliage, lending it a golden aura. In a Greek tale of the same name, Aeneas is instructed by a sibyl to pluck this plant before descending into the underworld, the explanation being it would both protect him on the journey and lend him confidence. He is guided to the sacred grove by two doves, symbols of the soul. If, again, Baldr is the 'beam' on which this mystic seedling grows then the two have a mutual relationship. Both would be hail and hearty and when the host dies, Baldr, the mistletoe dies with him; but all of this avoids the primary focus, which is a seiðr perspective.

Mistletoe is an extension of the eternal web, which is Baldr, who is All Hope, All Aspiration, the force and form of Truth and sacrifice. He is the path itself, the goal by which all things are created, journeyed, pursued beyond all resistance and confusion to a sun-filled and blessed goal. Baldr's role is that of enjoyment, what he shares with all that lives is gladness and gratification, merriment and mirth. He alone embodies all wealth and wisdom, all honor and glory, all sex and passion, all mægen and potential, all beauty and health, all pleasure and joy are his gifts to all beings. Baldr is more than Odin's son, more then the lineage of Jotuns; he somehow was transformed into the essence of space, the intermediary between chaos and cosmos. He had to die with the Age of Accord, at the cusp before Wolf Age begins, to be secreted away like a treasure is hidden from an assaulting horde, only to be revealed unharmed, the greatest of gifts, for the next Age of plenty on Midworld. This explains the magnificent and opulent reception awaiting him in Hella's Hall: she prepared the way for the sun to shine in Niflheim. As the sustainer of pure spirit, the divine sun, his presence has the ability to illumine even the darkest depths.

Little wonder mistletoe has become so fondly kept in Yule traditions. Even kissing under the mistletoe meant more than a show of affection but "Blessings be on you!" Its evergreen leaves and white to red berries - seiðr-wise, from semen to blood - became everlasting symbols of frith and fecundity; all due to its being a reflection of its host, Baldr.

~ ~ ~

Vol.33: *Alone had this plant to answer for the maiming, though greatly praised and decorated, being seen by all - vexed and baneful shaft - bringing risk and danger. Hod shot from a bow at his brother Baldr; Odin's son Váli born quickly, at one night old fighting [his brother's killer].*

Assuredly Baldr's death would be avenged, that a child but one day old would be the vindicator deserves an evaluation. Children are symbols of the future, the awakened forces of renewal that appear when great spiritual change, favorable change, is at the verge of manifestation. One day here vibrates with a similar pitch but with the added element of a mystical teacher or guide. It has been conjectured that 'hod' means blind or somehow, unseeing. Seiðr-wise his name has a quality of rash superiority and headlong temerity, behavior that certainly calls for realization, or the greater needs of community versus self-serving and brash acts. Váli then killed Hod not just to avenge Baldr, but so Hod could be re-aligned with multiversal laws.

~ ~ ~

Vol.34: *Nevertheless, he never took a hand to comb his hair - being the brave warrior he would never be free or at ease unless he fulfilled his task first; he was already aflame for a fight and ready to build a funeral pyre against Baldr's adversary. And Frigg did frown and decry this act at her Marshy Homestead, great danger now to the Slain's Hall! I go farther inward speaking, what more sensibility do you need?*

And Frigg did frown and decry this act at her Marshy Homestead. Marshes are places of decomposition, like swamps or peat bogs their energy is rich earth and water. From a seiðr perspective Frigg is the Dis of decomposing and decaying, of dormancy and rest, of life renewed and vibrancy. Frigg is Goddess of the Vernal Pools.

Vernal pools are vibrant examples of Midworld's ecosystem, of the successive and eternal threads of nature that she spins upon her seasonal distaff. From her hall, upon a gently sloping plain of grassland, rain flows in rivulets and is collected upon layers of clay. These reservoirs of hidden treasure are birthing grounds of new life and new meaning; from winter's wet eggs and spores, to spring's flowers and plants sprouting in dark moist soil, to summer/autumn's dry and cracking decay, and back again - her endless toiling is the promise of renewal. As the Sacred Sustainer of Life, a more beautiful example of ancestral truth and the preservation of heredity cannot be found.

On a seiðr journey this traveler saw men and women wearing the tusks of boars about their necks, some wore but one where others wore many. All of them had been painted green, like lichen. Their hair was plaited and green colored like young shoots of grass, and their clothing was green like new growth on dark rich soil. In silence they ate porridge made from grain-laced ergot, the only sound a cock's crow in the distance. The moon rose full over a marsh and all gathered walked, in trance, towards it. Upon reaching the marsh they touched its surface where the moon glow was, like an illumined pathway before them, and walking on the water's surface, upon the moon's reflection, a gentle humming was heard. It was like a whisper or delicate wisps of wind that coursed through all being, causing ripples and undulations within the soul. One by one they entered the marsh, humming softly; and upon reaching the center, slowly sinking downwards - with not a stir to the surface - their stark rich green covering merging with inky black. Watching still, after all had entered, the humming continued from every quarter equally as it came from within. This observer then recognized the humming as the soothing drone of a spinning wheel as it spun from death to life renewed. A profound sense of comfort swept over this seiðus' soul when it became clear that Frigg spins thread for the Norns; her loving hand a gift upon every wight as it becomes woven upon the Great Loom. The trance then ended.

Frigg's marshlands support the underworld; from both Lore and experience her realm is one of transition between land and water, between conscious and unconscious, between living and dead.

~ ~ ~

Vol.35: *From here I see the Wailing Vali, slaughtered, fighting, daring more against the hostility; strong he is against the troop who dares assault him. Bound and chained with fetters I saw, under Grotti, the Turning Wheel, lying there with proud temper was Loki, anchored in disgrace. There sits Victorious Delight, Sigyn, not able to revenge one against many; protecting her husband with her goodness, her duty and homage to him. I have demonstrated my consciousness to be existent and deep, to what end do you seek?*

Vali the Wailer, Loki's son is brutally murdered and his intestines pulled out and used to bind his father. Seiðr-wise Vali is the circumscriber and encloser, confiner and encircler, chieftain of dark forces who dwell in dark holes and caves, far from Sunna's vibrancy. Bowels are symbolic of the curved path or crooked road that some encounter en route to Hella's Hall; their energy is of containment, as in capturing or collecting. In other words, like Váli's murder of Hod, Vali's internal strength, his very guts, are used as a means of purifying Loki's disruptive behavior-character.

Bound and chained with fetters I saw, under Grotti, the Turning Wheel, lying there with proud temper was Loki, anchored in disgrace. Like Aurgelmir before him, perhaps Loki's bones will be ground to create sand and soil.

There sits Victorious Delight, Sigyn - not able to revenge one against many - protecting her husband with her goodness, her duty and homage to him. Sigyn, whose name means 'Victorious Delight', has powerful mægen: the fierce woman who stands by her man, duty-bound, expressing her deepest respect through vigilant deeds while contemplating revenge.

I have demonstrated my consciousness to be existent and deep, to what end do you seek? This is similar to strophe 34 where Gullveig-Heið is both asking and demanding to know how far and how deep Odin wishes for her to see. Odin does not have this skill - if he did there would be no need of her services - yet he impels and urges the völva inward and onward to either visions she has yet to experience personally, or simply has no interest in. Either way, Odin is deeply motivated by the events of Ragnorok and seemingly unsatisfied at this point with the answers already provided.

~ ~ ~

Vol.36: *It is not then unmet that from an isolated eastern mountain, surrounded by a venomous dale of daggers and swords, came Fierce- and Cruel-Sheath.*

The east represents spiritual illumination - a mountain that must be surmounted, even if difficult to arrive at. As obstacles, this destination is surrounded by a venomous dale of stagnant manifestation, by fields of daggers and swords, by strong emotions of revenge and death, all concealed within a cruel sheath or capsulized container. The summit is well worth achieving, it's the journey that is brutal.

~ ~ ~

Vol.37: *Pillars stood before the north, marking the Dark Moon Fields (where are found the mounds of* völva's). *Departed souls come out of there rich with gold from Sindar's family, him of the Sparking Iron-Scales. Deeper within are pillars of un-cold, where is found Jotun's beer hall, Dashing of Surf is called.*

Pillars stood before the north, marking the Dark Moon Fields (where are found the mounds of völva's). These northern pillars are animated with strength and the establishment of strength, of unity and justice, the plane on which they stand is a level foundation, one that creates stability; literally the middle ground of destruction and creation. The dark moon has the energy of stillness and calm, uninfluenced by waxing or waning energy, an excellent time for seiðus to journey.

Departed souls come out of there rich with gold from Sindar's family, him of the Sparking Iron-Scales. Deeper within are pillars of un-cold, where is found Jotun's beer hall, Dashing of Surf is called. Sindar's spark is the heat of each soul; he is, therefore, a Jotunic-soul father. The warm beer found here, close to ocean's dashing surf or purity, is the drink of life in that those who drink it feel like Tivar, if but for a moment. Otherwise, an excellent kenning for Jotun's Beer Hall: 'Surf'.

~ ~ ~

Vol.38: *I saw a homestead standing far from the sun; on the Woven Rope of Corpses there is a north-facing doorway. Poison falls in drops from a contentious opening, a private room above which is strong with snakes, very distressful, a sly and crooked place.*

From the sun denotes cold, darkness, and isolation. Opening to the north indicates Cron Huel or the Dark Wheel of Yule, winter solstice. Snakes have beautiful energy but also project sinister undulations of destruction and danger, they represent both individual and collective immorality. Nastrandir, the 'Woven Rope of Corpses' is a place, according to Lore, where perjurers and murderers dwell and are constantly strangled and gagged.

~ ~ ~

Vol.39: *I saw then, wading in a burdened stream, perjured men and murderous outlaws, and those who otherwise confuse the ear of a woman with false-intimacy. In this place, the Dark Biter, Nidhogg, defiles the forward wave of newly departed souls, and a strangler deceives existence. Inwardly I know these things; would you know more and what?*

Here exists a clear thought from our ancestors: Deliberate falsehood, murder, distortion, and beguiling behavior receive only pain.

~ ~ ~

Vol.40: *Eastwards sits an Old One in the Iron Forest - there feeding Fenris' kind; and it happens that one is fit above any other - the Lunar Year Destroyer - in troll shape.*

East is the point of origin and outcome, the place of beginnings (some may say the 'past', but beginnings are ever new). Strophe 36 mentions an "isolated eastern mountain", home, no doubt, to the Old One mentioned above, to whom a great deal of conjecture has been made. Many suggest this is none other than Angrboda, "Bidder, Messenger of Grief and Sorrow". As a 'messenger' it is reasonable that she would send a token to announce her arrival, perhaps in the form of a mistletoe arrow. Whoever this is their role is as caretaker-mother to Fenris and his kind. Feeding and caring for these beasts is a task few willingly take on; the only other example is Tiw, who lost his hand to keep that Oath.

According to Lore Loki had several children: Fenris of the Bog, Jörmungandr the Vast Monster, Hella - Mother of Death, Sleipnir, Vali the Wailer, Narfi the Corpse, and 'every ogress'; these first three are said to be had with Angrboda. (1) Because every hurt child seeks out the comfort of its mother, there is little doubt this is where Fenris fled, once free from gleipnir, to the only place of safety he knew: his mother's arms.

From this strophe there exists more then one great wolf but a pack of his 'kind', siblings or those who share similar attributes, perhaps even man-wolves or werewolves. (Fenris' brother Narfi was turned into a wolf, so surely, he would be here.) If so then Angrboda is a primal Wolf Mother.

Bear, wolf, and boar warriors are mentioned frequently in the Lore. Odin appears to be associated with both bears and wolves, though the berserkers, 'bear-shirts', or Bear Warriors seem to hold more of his favor. (2) Freyja, borrowing from her brother's beast Gullinbursti, perhaps 'feeds' her Boar Warriors. This would then consign the 'wolf leavings' - assuming the three should be accounted for - to the Old One of the Iron Wood, making Angrboda the powerful Wolf Mother-Warrior who is harboring and enriching a wolf band.

Angrboda's energy is unique in that she is a deadly trickster; unlike Loki who extends a deceitful hand - always faining trust - Angrboda's darkness is steady and open. Seiðr-wise, she dwells in a dark grove atop a bleak mountain ever shrouded in shade and mist. Her soft songs lure unsuspecting wanderers and hunters much like the Lorelei who brings loss and suffering. In appearance she is statuesque, her clothing covered in lichen. She has the ability to render all those who stumble upon her spiritually mute and soul-confused. Those who seek primal energy from the Gýgjar (female Jotuns) are wise to seek her cautiously. (3)

At your own risk, approach her in dark wild places with clothing worn inside out, sing a vardlokkur to her and bring a gift of suet mixed with grain, or of dark bread. Placing a staff upon the ground look east between your legs to view her true form. What she decides after this is based on the hard work, sincerity, and dedication of the (hopefully) well-seasoned seiðus' soul.

..Fenris' kind. Fenris means "of the bog", the symbology of which - in reference to Frigg - has already been discussed. His name sounds akin to Feronia, the Sabine Wolf Mother who ruled before Rome was built, and ferrum, the Latin word for 'iron'. (4)   Feronia is honored in February - Fébrua Lupa - with a great feast called the Lupercaly, a time to honor the Wolf Mother with hundreds of candles and lamps. Similar to Juno, Feronia brings illumination to the seeds of growth and renewal, as Juno-Fébrua she is the infernal goddess of spiritual rest after death. Roman slaves carried a statue of Ferônia Lupa through the streets, singing her praises as Goddess of Purification and Atonement, once their task was complete the bearers were granted freedom, in this case meaning the ultimate freedom of death. Feronia's Sabine priestesses were gifted with divine touch, or the ability to heal the sick, during full moons she spoke with them through an oracle, and during her annual festival her priestess' demonstrated their dedication by walking on burning coals.

From the earliest written records wolves have haunted the dreams of humans; clearly their strong imagery has endured as both protector and destroyer. Virgil, a Celt who became a poet of Roman, living in the 1st century BCE, wrote about mistletoe as a man-wolf repellent. Can this be part of Baldr's myth? Is there truth or deceit in tales that relate how dark women of death - who live with wild wolf packs on mountaintops - can relate primal knowledge and eternal wisdom? Perhaps the wolf beckons the soul to be more, to become world-wise, while never forgetting the primal undercurrent that forever stirs soul's existence. Odin's two wolves, Geri and Freki, represent, seiðr-wise, 'thirst' and 'hunger', reminding us to "Ever thirst for knowledge, ever hunger for wisdom". (5)

World lore is in virtual agreement regarding the beneficial nature of wolves. There are countless examples of gods and heroes who are swallowed whole by serpents, bears, or wolfs, acting as facilitators of rebirth or spiritual transformation. Therefore, couldn't the above reference, and many more like it in Northern European lore, signify the same idea?

Tribal folk generally regard all life as sacred, sensing a deep sacred affinity with all that lives. A wolf exhibits impeccable skills of survival and hunting, attributes that would have been readily noticed, equally so its tendency to unfailingly care for its litter and kin, even showing compassion for those outside its pack; clearly a powerful symbol of greatness in our midst. It was only later, when the warrior tribes became settled - farming and raising animals behind fences - that the wolf became a threat-competition, part of the utgart.

Like berserkers, 'bear-shirt' wearers, humans are able of being ulfhednir or ulfhamr, or taking on a wolf form (among others). From *Vatnsdæla Saga*, "Those berserkir who were called ulfhednir had got wolf-skins over their mail coats." Perhaps this transition, from vital fighting element to agrarian society, was difficult for those individuals with innate warrior attributes. Initially these folk were admired for their fighting prowess, their ability to bring an overall sense of security to their kinsmen - a vital tool in both war and seiðr - but when no longer need, this ability created fear and dread. After all, there was no longer a need to prowl about in wolf's clothing (or bear, or boar for that matter). Seiðr-wise this marks a cutting of the thread between Folksoul and folk-memory. It would seem that around this time the word vargr, 'wolf', started to take on a double meaning, one of outlaw.

There exists the *hamr*, or original shape, alongside another shape, the *eigi einhamir*, 'not of one skin'; meaning, there are two bodies, two natures, both ready to be recognized and assumed. *Skipta hömum* is the ability to transition - a technique passed to this seiðu from a grandsire - or skinskipt. Once this new shape is 'put on' it is able to *hamför* or 'fare-forth', a vital seiðr tool in that *hamramr* is but one way personal mægen becomes strengthened.

The exact way of skinskipting or shape-shifting is not the focus of this commentary; suffice it to say there are several ways to go about it that result in three forms of skin-shifting. (6) Briefly, the three forms are: touching - when one soul is transferred to the body of another for a brief moment; dreaming - where the physical form appears dead; skipting - the existence of two physical forms, one human and one animal. The second form is generally done while wearing a cloak or fur, the latter, assuredly, is the most difficult and dangerous, and commonly referred to as *gandreid*.

However, wolves do not always represent sacred transformation, the *Atharva Veda* lists the wolf - with five other animals - as one of the six 'mind foes', or psychological obstacles; the wolf, in particular, representing anger. (7) According to ancient Greek lore, Hecate, the Goddess of Death and Witchcraft, has a pack of wolves that she hand-feeds 'warm flesh'; and Chiron, the Ferryman, has, literally, wolf ears.

'Wolf' is one of the many loan words from our Indo-European cousins. (8) In strophe 40 above the word vargr-wolf, has been rendered 'outlaw' and 'strangler' based on the verse reference to criminals. One of the penalties for such a criminal being strangulation, a punishment associated with Odin as the Hangaguth: "Easy to recognize for all who come there is Odin's lofty hall: the wolf lurks before the west door, the eagle hovers above." - *Grimnismal* 10. This could possibly explain why Fenris kills Odin, not Tiw, as a symbol of sacred transformation - he is repaying Odin for a punishment received. *Wearg*, meaning 'scoundrel; fiend', is the Anglo-Saxon term for outlaws, further seen in the Norman laws where final sentencing for certain offences was the verdict: Wargus esto! ("Be an outlaw!"). Later still the European Catholic church used wolves - in the form of werewolves or men who are transformed into mindless animals after signing a pact with the devil - to sow fear during the inquisition; in one particular circumstance, the werewolves were actually 'heroes' and 'warriors'. (9)

For 'good' or 'bad' wolfs have remained imbedded in folk-memory, even found frequently in noble birth names. For example: Radulf, Ralph, and Randall are German, and Scandinavian Rafer means, 'wolf counsel.' Ulrika is both Old German and Old English for 'wolf ruler', while Ulva is Teutonic for 'she-wolf, brave'. Radolf, Radolph, Raedwolf, Raff, and Ralf are English meaning, 'red wolf.' Rafe, Randal, and Randon are English, Ranolf and Ranulfo are Teutonic, and Anglo-Saxon Rand, all mean, 'shield wolf.' Rafer is Scandinavian for 'wolf', and Randolph is English for, 'house wolf; protector'

..in the Iron Forest. Iron has long been held as a sacred object, more so iron meteorites - the seeds of creation - that fall as gifts from heaven. Usually found as lumps upon the ground, iron - thought to be falling stars

- was treated with respect and sometimes worshipped. (10) The Temple of Diana contained an object said to be a *"symbol of her which fell from heaven"*, just as there are references for other such sacred objects throughout the ancient world. (11) Ancient Egyptians considered 'sky-iron', which was mostly black and often cone-shaped, to be the "bones" of star-gods. (12) Working with meteorites brought this seiðr worker to the conclusion that these were primally considered as 'thunderbolts.'

Closer to Heathenry, in circumpolar shamanic lore the Pole Star, or 'nail of heaven', is said to be a rod made of celestial iron.

- the Lunar Year Destroyer. Often translated as 'to snatch the sun' or 'to destroy the sun', this strophe actually reads: *tungls tjúgari*, 'moon destroyer.' As already pointed out, the author's specialty is not Old Norse but seiðr, even so, it is difficult to add a word where one does not exist, equally as it is to subtract one that does.

Historically time has been reckoned in lunations, the night being a point of reference. Due to the moon's phases, an ever-changing object in the night sky, this is understandable. In conjunction with this there are the solstices and equinoxes, which were determined by the nearest new or full moon, and worked to neatly divide the lunar year. The difference between a lunar calendar and a solar one (the latter being a model for the current Gregorian configuration) is eleven days. These became known as intercalary days, or extra days, and served to 'balance' the year, so to speak. Seiðr-wise, these extra days are set aside as a seiðr tide, or holy days for seiðus.

The Julian Calendar, adopted in 46 BCE, didn't work for those who retained the folk memory and sacred traditions of the moon year, for them the lunar calendar continued for another one thousand plus years. Traditionally, a month was from one full moon to the next, approximately 29.5 days. The difference between the solar and lunar is further seen in the three 'seasons' of our Northern European ancestors - a solar year is twelve months divided into four seasons while the lunar year is thirteen months divided into three seasons with four months each. (13) In the northern regions sun is due south at noon and at night the Pole Star points due north, this made navigation fairly accurate.

Time today is far different then how our ancestors understood it. Today we measure time with atomic cloaks dividing it into hours, minutes, and seconds; our forebears recognized units of night and day - sunrise, midday, and sunset, wax and wane of the moon - and the movement of stars in the sky, whose distinct brightness was a reliable means of determining or forecasting, as they still are today. These events, plus flood and famine, for example, were also annotated. Our ancestors observed the heavens, primarily the sun, moon, and stars (perhaps relating back to strophe 25 and Freyja), to discover and so work intimately with the terrestrial and celestial rhythms. Throughout Northern Europe there exist standing stones and astronomical markers built to mark the solstices, equinoxes, and cross-quarter days, which brings this verse commentary back to wolves and their relationship to the lunar year.

Sirius is the most recognizable star on Midworld, seen by every inhabited region on earth, particularly in the Northern Hemisphere. There are two optimum times for viewing Sirius in the northern and southern hemispheres: at the winter and summer solstices (the latter being the 'dog days of summer', or a mystic metaphor, in this instance). Considered the 'opener of the year' in both hemispheres, Sirius heralds the lunar year. Seiðr-wise this is the mystery of the Midnight Sun (another mystic metaphor), or the coming forth into the multiverse's first day, for at midnight the Wolf Star reaches its meridian, marking a new generation of the earth.

Among Indo-Europeans the month of the summer solstice was known as *Tir*, which means, "star". (According to current reckoning this would be June, when Sirius - the dog or wolf star - rises.) For the ancient Egyptians, Tir brought rain and the annual rising of the Nile River, their calendar being centered on this event. In ancient Persia during the month of Tir-Tishtryehe, they celebrated the Tir-agan Feast, which heralded summer rains and new life.

This coming of rain - a stirring of wind-air like a cosmic cauldron - creates clouds that are, to the experienced seiðu, bearers of spirit. Further, the rains of Sirius take on three forms: seed-rain - that fertilizes the fields; warrior-rain - which thrashes the grain loosening the husk; and Tir-rain - spirit-rain that gives birth to food for the nourishment of all that lives.

Tyr-Tiw is the Pole Star, the tail-star of Ursa Minor, the most important star to navigators of wide seas and open plains, the Guiding Light that ever watches. This particular pole is not fixed but has long been observed to be migrating north. In 2,105 ACE, for example, Tiw's Eye will rest and be centered on the North Celestial Pole, and previously, in 3,000 BCE, this point was the 'tail' of Draco, and finally, in 5,000 years hence, the Pole

Star will be Alderamin, the brightest star in the constellation Cepheus. So, currently, Midworld is under the watchful eye and influence of Tiw's Pole Star.

Tiw's Pole Star - his spear - is known by many names: Steering Star, Ship Star, North Star, Dog's Tail, Star of the Sea, Dog's Tail, and Lodestar. When Óð, Vili, and Ve sculpted Aurgelmir's body to form Midworld they affixed their creation in place with the *Veralder Nagli*, or World Nail, forever threading the sky to earth. This is akin to Sámi Tribes who see the "Golden Peg" as the point that holds the universe together, just as the ancient astronomers of India knew this same point as the "Pivot of the Planets."

For our northern European relations, Sirius emerges in the harshest of dark winter, illuminating the cold skies, marking the exact same spot where the sun will appear at dawn, which is the principal tide of the northern European tribes. For this seiðr scholar, this means that Sirius, the Wolf Star, Fenris himself, is forever tethered to Tiw, the Pole Star - which is Tiw's Oath to all that lives.

Tiw-Pole Star, forged of cosmic-iron, is forever threaded to Fenris-Wolf Star, the two bound by cord and hand. This cord a thread that connects every realm of existence, the hand one of strength and protection, that together forever entwine to create a conscious and tangibly protective center that weaves humanity into the realms of all existence. Or, ever assuring that the Great Beast is tethered to the Iron Nail of heaven, unable to harm Midworld.

- *in troll shape.* Beyond doubt this wolf is an ill-disposed monster, ready to destroy the human race.

Reference
(1) And 'every ogress.' Reference: *Hyndluljod.* More accurately, this is rendered 'evil woman.'

(2) Bear Warriors. From 156 names of Odin, as found in *Norse Myth and Legend,* two (2) of those names reference bears, and one (1) references a wolf. From 235 names of Odin, as found on:
http://www.angelfire.com/on/Wodensharrow/odennamn.html,
four (4) of those names reference wolves and two (2) reference bears.

(3) Gýgjar. "Giantess; hag", female Jotuns.

(4) Sabine Wolf Mother. Many scholars relate the Wana to the Sabine tribes.

(5) Ever hunger for wisdom. Geri and Freki are 'thirst' and 'hunger', the physical aspect of being, whereas Hugn and Munin are 'thought' and 'memory', the emotive-intellectual aspect of being. Both references are from *Yngonamal*.

(6) Skinskipting. Skipt, 'to divide in two'.

(7) Representing anger. *Atharva Veda* 8.4.22: owl-delusion, wolf-anger, dog-jealousy, phoenix-lust, eagle-arrogance, and vulture-greed.

(8) Indo-European cousins. Other examples, from *In Search of the Indo-Europeans*; J.P. Mallory:
- Trees and Plants: apple, ash, aspen, beech, corn, linden, oak, pine, and tree;
- Animals: bear, deer, otter, and wolf;
- Body parts: foot, head, heart, and lung;
- Nature: air, cold, mind, moon, night, snow, star, sun, and winter;
- Other: be, eat, father, honey, lie, long, mead, mother, red, sew, weave, and yoke; all clearly indicative of 'home' and therefore 'culture.'

(9) Werewolves. Reference: *Geography of Witchcraft*; M. Summers; New Jersey; 1963; Chapter 7 - Italy. Specifically the Benandanti Werewolves, lupo manero, were men who transformed themselves into wolves and traveled to the Underworld where they engaged in violent battles against evil witches. These men were considered heroes and brave warriors, responsible for saving their community.

(10) Worshipped. Reference: *Cosmic Debris - Meteorites in History*; J.G. Burke; 1986; throughout.

(11) Fell from heaven. The *Bible*, Acts 19:35.

(12) Star-gods. Reference: *The Pyramids of Egypt*; I.E.S. Edwards; 1979; pages 284-5.

(13) Three 'seasons'. These three seasons further correlated to the three major tides, or festivals, of the year, not the six or eight commonly considered today. These three seasonal holy times are: winter solstice,

summer solstice, and vernal equinox. Reference: *The Pagan Religions of the Ancient British Isles - Their Nature and Legacy*, by: R. Hutton; 1991; pages 59-60, and 285-6

~ ~ ~

Vol.41: *Filled with death's struggle he comes, beyond rescue he wishes for death; rust-colored, seeking only evil, his home is an iron bog oozing with blood. And it comes to pass that the sun is wounded, its shine becomes withered and summer cannot be found; ill-natured is the wind from that quarter. I am skilled! What more would you know!*

The Lunar Year Destroyer comes - there is no rescue from him, and no safe place. From the stench of boiling blood he casts his eye upon Sunna, she turns inward, casting a cloak between her and foul death. Summer is not found as the winds buffet Midworld obscuring all in reddened darkness. (1) These are dark days and barren nights.

Reference
(1) Summer is not found. This tide, Summer Finding, is just that: finding the summer, or guiding her back home, assuring her safe return benefits all that lives.

~ ~ ~

Vol.42: *Sitting there on the burial cairn, playing a harp with sly cunning, sits gleaming and golden Eggther, bodyguard and caretaker to the Gýgjar. The fine and light-red gallows cock crows from the goose-wood, Fjalarr he is called.*

Here is yet another example of burial mounds as places of sitting-out, similar to Gullveig-Heið from the first strophe. The musical reference here specifically mentions a harp (hörpu), an indication that this may have been used in seiðr. An often-quoted reference from *Lokasenna* 24 depicts Odin playing a "drum." The word in question there is *drápa*, meaning: "a heroic laudatory poem with refrains in the central portion". If this were the case, then connecting Odin to a 'shamanic drum' would be inaccurate. (1) Another translation of this verse could read: *"But you seemed to be uttering seiðr within Saamiland, and speaking poems in that place - at a shrine there upon the ground. As a pleasing wizard you passed over earth, taking an interest in that which has an unmanly nature."* "Speaking poems", or "chant", is kvæði, which is used more frequently when

90

referring specifically to seiðr. Suggestively then, the above strophe could reference an example of vardlokkur accompanied to harp music. Anyroad, there is little doubt regarding the Finno-Ugric use of drums during shamanic work, the question is: "Did the Northern Europeans borrow the Sámi drum for seiðr, or find an instrument more attune to their own culture, folk-memory, and spiritual vibration?"

..sits gleaming and golden Eggther. Many have rendered this 'glad Edge-dweller'. Utilizing the Indo-European root it translates as: 'gleam, shine; gold', which would make Eggther a 'golden useful egg'. Directly, 'egg' is the only word in English to end in -gg, and is also the same word in Old Norse (and Icelandic). From the Finnish national epic, the *Kalevala*, there is mention of seven eggs - six of gold and one of iron, that once hatched, formed all of heaven and earth. (2)

..bodyguard and caretaker to the Gýgjar. Eggther, a container of spiritual light, is guardian to the Gýgjar, or female Jotuns. (3) Eggs are containers for matter and thought, for hidden or occulted things, which, in this example, contains primal female energy. For the well-developed seiðr practitioner, this may be an inner core of mystery awaiting discovery.

The Gýgjar are powerful entities - wild and primitive, encompassing and devouring - mad women who carry the potential of all life. Soaring through space, traversing all realms, they are turbulent energy, crazy wisdom, and hysterical omnipotence. Not for the tame of heart or those who seek a subtle path towards seiðr penetration, for the Gýgjar offer a whirlwind of death and dismemberment, timelessness and formlessness.

Eggther is the repository for these forceful women, a brilliant receptacle of origin for the Gýgjar - who are without-origin, without-form; and like the breakable egg, his albumin is fragile and easily dissolved (like land holding back a hurricane). For those who study the symbology of seiðr, his attributes are keen examination into the foundational threads of individual life, the discontinuation of all that is ignoble within being; meaning to unweave all that has been woven, to become de-threaded. Then, with strength only acquired from dedication and commitment, the reweaving can begin - so the Three Are Made One.

The fine and light-red gallows cock crows from the goose-wood, Fjalarr he is called. According to Lore there are two cocks, one above and one below; their primordial screams alert all worlds to the inevitable creation and destruction. Today, cocks are found on weather vanes because a 9th

91

century pope thought it appropriate. Prior to this, gods and other animals of lore graced these intricate and practical devices. Being a 'gallows cock' Fjalarr's role is to 'awaken' those who 'hang' between the worlds - isolated, levitating lost souls affixed to their own dogma-doctrine, wandering the outskirts of Helheim. Fjalarr is the Beguiler and a deceiver, as a gallows cock he inflicts spiritual sickness and blindness, his angry energy is hungry for bloody sacrifice.

The 'goose-wood' here, often rendered 'bird-wood', is appropriate for the egg reference. (4) Geese represent descent into the Underworld, equally with the 'great mother'. More in relation to this strophe, the goose is linked with self-created destiny, or that which is meant to occur based on past deeds. (5)

Combined, a profound message is woven into this strophe. Exclusively, paying heed to primal forces with song and verse enriches and illumines the golden treasure within, empowering the seiðu to be released from the impressions of time and space (earth and heaven) and in so doing free themselves from death (and if not careful, bring about ignorance and illness). Could this also be the message for Odin, a message Gullveig-Heið repeats often, challenging him to extend his understanding further: Do you understand yet?

Reference
1) Drum. Reference: *Return of the Völva: Recovering the Practice of Seidh*; by: D. Paxson; article. Quote: "A passage from the Lokasenna is of especial interest, since if the verb in the second line is examined carefully, it may provide evidence for Norse use of the shamanic drum. Taunting Odin, Loki says -
But thou in Samsey wast performing Seidh
And beating out (spells) like a Völva,
Vitki-like didst pass through the world of men,
In woman's wise, I believe.
- (Lokasenna: 24)"
As an aside, Patricia Terry's translation offers this particular line as: "who murdered by magic".

(2) Heaven and earth. Reference: *Kalevala*, Runo 1.

(3) Female Jotuns. Further, reference J. Blain in *Nine Worlds of Seid-Magic* where she mentions how Rauðhildr and D. Paxon refer to these entities as 'Maunir'.

(4) 'Goose-wood'. Gaglviði; gagl means 'small goose'.

(5) The 'great mother'. Reference: J. Grimm's *Teutonic Mythology*, Vol 1; Gloucester; 1976; page 269

~ ~ ~

Vol.43: *Crows Golden-Comb over the gods, rousing from sleep those free-born who dwell with the Father of Hosts. Yet before that, the other roars from beneath earth, a loathsome and destructive cock in Hella's Hall.*

Raising upwards like a crescendo the first battle cry is quickly responded to by Gullinkambi's alarm to Odin's army. This increase of intensity - ascending from below to above - is an escalation from gross to sublime, representing the ability to soar above the human condition to achieve a cosmic or spiritual perspective. Fjalarr's spiritual sickness spiraling upwards towards Gullinkambi's divine intelligence moves from distress and anarchy to frith and Law. This, then, is the heart of Völuspá.

This verse commentary gravitates on Völuspá as a mystical text, one that illuminates the nature of seiðr, which is a spark of the exceptional flame, the unseen force that moves sun, moon, and stars. (1) All is simplicity - actually quite commonplace: the assertion of Folksoul against shadowless existence, or innangart versus utgart. As the opposition to bane this is the balefire of hope. Seiðr is the assertion of individual freedom against terror and temptation, it is absolute resistance to baseness, the most perfect of all oaths. Seiðr reveals the true worlds, but more importantly it reveals Midworld's treasure. More than an enclosure, a protective barrier against the unknown, our ancestors knew Midworld as the manifestation of the multiverse. All worlds, all realms reside within Midworld, which in turn manifests as human form, the bodymind-soul.

Ragnarök, God's Doom, is aroused courage, the slow rise of blood to boiling felt in our being during heroic moments; and this sensation is distinctly Heathen. It is the compelling awareness that drives us onwards to sacrifice all we are - for defeat to primal chaos is not failure but pristine rebirth and profound wisdom earned. Our greatest strength is that we, as a folk, cannot be destroyed.

Reference
(1) Seiðr .. spark of. A poetic definition. The definition used throughout this verse commentary is: a penetration of consciousness to access the spiritual multiverse, or trance.

~ ~ ~

Vol.44: *Now with building violence Garm stands before the great door of Highest Cave - remembering when the rope broke and the wolf ran free. I have great learning - powerful charms to assist me - for further still I see guilt fall: God's Doom! So to battle, you Gods of Victory!*

Now with building violence Garm stands before the great door of Highest Cave - remembering when the rope broke and the wolf ran free. There are two scenarios here: that Garm ("dog") and the wolf (possibly Fenris) is the same beast, or they are pack brothers-siblings. The verse, as written, indicates the two as identical, and indeed, dog and wolf often are in older texts. Determining either one or two is not the intent of this verse commentary, but the energy patterns behind the symbols.

Dogs are often portrayed as companions to the dead, accompanying them to Hella's Hall, for instance. Equally, they are guardians who assure none enter that do not belong. It would seem then that there exists a wild beast, the wolf, who will destroy the sun - life as we know it - and a tame beast, the dog, who accompanies us to the next realm of existence; both the bringer of destruction and the guide along the way. 'Don't bite the hand that feeds you' is a mystic metaphor here: when the light of life is extinguished it can be rekindled, therefore, it is wise to remember those who have fueled the flame of both life and death, for there cannot be one without the other.

I have great learning - powerful charms to assist me - The völva is asserting her authority, making it clear that her vision is greater than Odin's.

..for further still I see guilt fall: God's Doom! So to battle, you Gods of Victory! This strophe resembles a goading, a prompt to finish the pattern created up to this moment; for after all, there is no other destiny then that which is hand-woven.

~ ~ ~

Vol.45: *Brothers will beat and bring death to each other, cousins will be spoiled by adultery; there is difficulty in the world and great whoredom. Shield Age, Axe Age: shields - discernment and knowledge are trapped and torn asunder. Wind Age, Wolf Age: already the world is degraded and overthrown. No memory will remain of man being reverent, of showing respect, to another.*

Shield Age, Axe Age - shields, as discernment and knowledge, are trapped and torn asunder. Shields are symbolic of spiritual defense and axes are primal strength and origins, combined these two represent a period of enlightenment, a divine renaissance now lost.

Wind Age, Wolf Age - already the world is degraded and overthrown. Wind is tumultuous and disruptive and wolves the unknown darkness, combined these two represent a period of decay and violence, the discord before destruction.

No memory will remain of man being reverent, of showing respect, to another. The spiritual life is forgotten, there exists no memory of the unity of Midworld - of how it exists in human form. 'Man' is the connecting link, the vital principal between all realms - a wisdom now lost so that none respects the other, not seeing in the other soul-seeds of profound life.

~ ~ ~

Vol.46-47: *Plays Mim at denial, but the measure of doom is against this guiling kin - soon struck down by Screaming Horn - for it happens that Heimdallr's horn of defense is held aloft. Shaken by the sound, Yggdrasil's Ash stands, the Tree of Life groaning; Odin speaks to Mim's greatness, and the Jotun is set free. Come the dreadful on Hella's Road, Surt leading the way, those of like-mind swallowing all before them.*

Deception and deceit are aspects of the mind, all self-imposed; dark sorceries that many fall prey to, certainly something seiðus must ward against. Heimdallr's horn emits pure sound, a divine octave that tears asunder all arrogance, a vibration so great that the Great Yew is shaken - the human form. Odin addresses the wisdom of mind (as opposed to its folly); even so, primordial chaos is released. Those that come from

Hella's Road are not the ancestors, our blood relations, but Jotuns and Trolls, dark-forces whose nature it is to break down life.

Surt's energy is the "Jotun .. set free" here; interpretations of this line consider either Loki or Fenris, but Surt's fire - his black all-consuming flame that levels existence - alone hearkens the God's Doom. Nor are these ordinary flames, but fire of mind - the un-evolved, imperfect spiritual ignorance that can only lead to spiritual wisdom.

Ragnarök presents the seiðu with yet another trinity, similar to those already considered, Óð-Vili-Ve and Urd-Verdandi-Skuld, and like these previous examples nothing exists outside of them, for they are fundamentally that simple. (1) This new trinity is Ginnunga-gap, Frey, and Surt, or, that which is *Above Time*, *Against Time*, and *In Time*, respectively; and as is the case in all trinities, they weave one rope - the Three Made One.

Heathenry has no single creator but an indefinable viable nothingness, a vast expanse of being and no-being, of darkness and no-darkness, of death and no-death, of the breathless breath. Ginnunga-gap is unexplainable. Its energy is dark light without end, pooling and swirling spheres that wax and wane, magnificent sound - divine utterances, primal galdr - that create, sustain, and destroy all that lives. It is uncreated because human minds cannot conceive of it. It is the primal pulse and impulse of galdr, both soft hum and thunderous crash, gentle song and terrifying scream. It is purest potential and probability, the birther of chaos, or that which exists prior to organization, before time. All that emanates from the Gap, and though 'created' by it, remains distinct from it, meaning its outpourings maintain their originative form. It is no-time, eternal, and *Above Time*.

Frey is an original form, that of World Sustainer or the fecundity of all that lives. His energy is found in everyman as the desire to create in their own likeness, or the will to remain the same, unchanged, ever longing to be timeless or *Against Time*. Frey is the force and form of all life, an energy current that, like a trailing vine, ever seeks the sun's rays, or a return to balance and original beauty.

Surt is no enemy to Tivar or wight but a primal force of nature (unlike frost Jotuns which are absolute uncontrollable chaos). Where Frey is the green-vegetative world, Surt is either the warming hearth fire or the blaze that levels a home. His is a necessary darkness, much like a volcano - ever destructive yet leaving behind new land. The dead reach Hella's Hall through Surt for he is the Jotun of funeral pyres, the flesh-eater and purifier. Surt is a messenger who conveys all sacrifices to their proper destination.

Fledgling seiðus should be mindful of a fire's direction: fire in the north for all wights, in the east for the Tivar, in the south for cooking and mooting, and west for the dead.

Surt exudes golden energy (his attire) and readily accepts gold gifts from those who respect him. Surt's nature is felt in Sunna's heat and Thor's lightening bolt, in the warmth of human skin and the aura it generates, the vitality and virility of life itself. He is passion and perfection, temper and rage. (2) Surt is nauthiz, the friction created when two sticks are rubbed together, the need fire.

Surt's name is rooted in 'black'-ness - as the leader of Muspelsheim, Home of Fire - his life's essence is the throbbing phenomenal existence that ever turns the Great Wheel of Manifestation. (3) It is his task to plunge all that lives into unimaginable flame so that nothing remains but Ginnunga-gap. All realms, all stars and planets, all galaxies and universes, every blade of grass and every birdsong will be enveloped in a vast sea of fire; an Ocean of Flame that returns all form-matter back to primordial, fiery, and spiritual nature. As World Destroyer, or that energy pattern that desires change above all else, he blazes the way for temporary disintegration. As the greatness of time he is *In Time*, a time that draws all realms - even the nine realms of creative energy - to their inevitable conclusion; all must be destroyed in order to be re-formed.

Without Surt there would be no Golden Age, for only in destruction are things made anew, therefore, he is the connecting link back to Ginnunga-gap. As the essence of destruction he can only evolve forward, or what some may consider the 'future'. And if there is any doubt of this, then look to his tool of destruction, the weapon he wields for purification and transformation is the mighty and fecund sword of Frey.

Surt is the Lunar Death Destroyer of strophe 40 who is released during Cron Huel, the Dark Wheel of Yule. Sky wise, at the end of Bifrost (the Milky Way) lies Muspelsheim (the southern horizon), from where will come the fierce dogs, the great devourers - Loki unbound (Canis Major) and Surt blazing forward (Canis Minor). From this direction comes Ragnarök, from the constellation Auriga, the "Wagoner".

It would be easy here to see Thor as this Wagoner, especially since Auriga is related to goats, however, exclusively, this is Baldr, the first growth after Frey and Surt - who are innate life-force and absolute destruction. Baldr's role then, which will be explored yet again in strophes 61 and 62, is that of harmonious weaver of the trinity, the 'smoother' of the way, a brilliant light of multiversal Truth.

There exists in Heathenry no better example of the life-eternal Law of constant change away from, of untiring aspiration towards, and ceaseless effort back to original perfection and the ineffable inner peace of timelessness - forever inseparable - then these three. For all of life must be destroyed, all darkness snuffed out, for Law and Troth to rule on Midworld.

Reference

(1) Trinity. Another trinity is that of Rita, Tiw, and Tisa. Tisa-Zisa is Earth Mother to Tiw's Sky Father - she is a primal creatrix. Combined, Tiw and Tisa are inseparable primordial cosmos. Only Rita, the keeper of divine order and the mover of all planets - gravity itself - demarcates them. Rita is the Coverer, the bringer of cosmic order; one of his sons is Mani, keeper of time on Midworld. Rita is lord of the dead who are past Hella's Hall, and has the ability to confer immortality. Tisa is the dawn and the plow, a cow's first milk and a baby's first cry for mother; she receives all those who die with alluvial acceptance.

(2) Thor's lightening bolt. Exclusively, Surt's brother, perhaps twin to Thor.

(3) Great Wheel of Manifestation. This is Grotti, which is akin to the Great Wheel of Un-manifestation, or Ginnunga-gap.

~ ~ ~

Vol.48: *Consider the Gods, consider the Alfar - all of Jotunheim is clashing! The gods have assembled, dwarves - sprouting from steep rock - groan at the stone door. Should I reveal more or what?*

Exclusively, Alfar are vibrant star energy grounded in earth, enduring symbols that are older than Tivar and Jotuns, for they hail from the heavens beyond heaven. They are the Golden Race, the Star Race, who came to earth like meteorites and have remained ever since (which is why some consider them to be 'angels').

Suggestively, as master skinskipters, they often appear in animal form, favoring birds and horses, but will also shape themselves into half-human and half-animal shapes; likewise they can be incredibly small, quite huge, or appear as wind or water, for example. Highly skilled in music and dance they are the bringers of lyrical instruments, sacred song, and wind-like dance movements - either gentle or frantically wild. Memory of them has lingered in folk memory as the Huldre, but loosely.

Intuitively, they are associated with burial mounds, their strength coming from decomposition and decay; therefore they are the composters of life and restorers of fertility or what some may refer to as 'nature spirits', or náttúrur. Exclusively, after Óð, Vili, and Ve formed Midworld from Aurgelmir's form, it was the Alfar who fashioned and crafted the rough edges; which is why they are often associated with beautiful things. As beings of earth and nature they have impeccable hearing and bring stability to life.

Assumptively, those families they favor are gifted at birth with Luck. As personal attendants of the highest vibration they are embodiments of hamingja. Some may refer to them as Disir, and though often projecting female energy they are genderless. Aside from humans, they affix themselves to natural features like wells and old trees, mountains and waterfalls, granting gifts to those who assist them in preserving such sites. These entities are impeccable allies for seiðus.

~ ~ ~

Vol.49: *Now, with great mastery does Garm stand before the Highest Cave. The fastener is removed - torn asunder - greed runs free. Much have I helped you, teaching what I know, further still comes God's Doom - to battle, you Gods of Victory!*

~ ~ ~

Vol.50: *Old Age Sickness comes from the east with linden-tree raised high. Waves are beaten by serpent turning; the Vast-Great Monster churns Jotun-wrath; then, eagles screaming tears asunder pale waning moon. Nail Ship is set free!*

Hrym is 'Old Age Sickness', interesting that he holds aloft a linden-shield, symbol of immortality and access to the higher realm of consciousness.

99

Exclusively, this reference links to the Sámi shamans, who our ancestors are said to have trained with to supplement their mystic knowledge. Lindens are central to shamanic rites and have a wide symbolic range.

From the *Mabinogion*, this day is marked as one of vengeance, where Llew, Bright One of the Skillful Hand, kills Goronwy with a Sunlight Spear. According to Welsh lore, Llew and Goronwy are twin gods of light and dark, the god of light always being born or restored-reborn at Cron Huel, the Winter Solstice. Then, at Sol Huel, the "Sun's Wheel" or Summer Solstice, his 'Wyrd' twin is born, and the only time when one can 'kill' the other - when light is able to conquer dark and dark to conquer light - is at the equinoxes. In the above strophe, Hrym has become old, he is decrepit darkness, and ready to ascend or make way for the fire or light to come, represented by the linden-tree-shield.

If there is a correlation between these myths, then Llew is astrological Leo, betrayed by his wife Blodeuwedd, astrological Virgo, struck down but not killed, instead transformed into an eagle, or astrological Scorpio. (1) Combined with the other symbols here, the Wagon drawn by goats - astrological Cancer and Capricorn, or summer and winter - places these events between the two solstices.

Lindens are often depicted with 'golden crowns' and 'silver trunks', and indeed they do have this appearance. Exclusively, this tree represents Baldr, god of the new dawn (Vernal Equinox) and the Underworld; Hella did, after all, hold a great feast upon his arrival. Additionally lindens are associated with 'under' or hidden, possibly indicating two realms where the dead congregate: Hella's Hall, the Underworld, and Ran's Hall, the Waterworld.

Waves are beaten by serpent turning; the Vast-Great Monster churns Jotun-wrath. Pure force, plan and simple - that is what Jörmungandr is. Its every movement, from hissing to shedding, is equivocated to something else, for either 'good' or 'bad'. Similar to Gnostic lore where the serpent is seen biting its tail, Jörmungandr too is a beast so vast it encircles the earth, therefore creating a circle. Or, all things ambivalent - the right and wrong, the healing and harmful, the constructive and destructive, it seems there is no middle ground with such beasts (literally). Suggestively, perhaps Jörmungandr, 'earth's wand', is the equator.

Serpents are found the world over, living beneath the sea and on mountain tops, hiding in trees and under rocks, they are seen as tiny and harmless to giant dragons breathing fire and destroying entire villages. Seiðr-wise the offspring of Jörmungandr appear as half-human and half-snake and are the maintainers of Ley Lines or Worm Trails, those electro-magnetic currents that criss-cross all realms of existence and afford travel to those who know how to enter and exit them. Especially those master seiðus who commune with the wise-serpent entities.

..eagles screaming tears asunder pale waning moon. Eagles represent the first light of day, here it is seen 'tearing asunder' the moon or night. A new day is dawning, a new world.

Nail Ship is set free! Nails are used to affix an object to a particular place. A well-known example are the regin-nails said to be used in Hof's, where the 'god pillars' reside; perhaps assuring the gods are affixed to a particular abode or location. Circumpolar shamans refer to the Pole Star as a nail, an object that affixes the heavens to the earth. Ships are certainly symbols of movement, from one place or realm to another. A ship of nails, a Nail Ship, would then denote a fixed location, a central point in which other things move around it. This unvarying mean is nothing less then the cause of all change.

Like Grotti - the Great Turning Wheel of seasons, of stars in the heavens, of life transformations - there are wheels upon wheels in every life and those who seek the center, or hub. Seiðus purposely, deliberately seek this sacred central point, the permanence that never changes; for in the center, all perspectives are readily seen. Like a spider's web, where even the tiniest of ripples is felt in the center, so that nothing goes by unnoticed. There is then, no one better to guard and protect the innermost well-being of community then the mature seiðu who stands calm and far-seeing.

Reference
(1) Scorpio. An alternate symbol for Scorpio is the eagle.

~ ~ ~

Vol.51: *Ship journeys from the north, steered and ruled over by Loki. Coming with surety are Hella's great host of men - with very severe monsters - to establish her laws; and to these, that brother Bee-Sock, in company to attack.*

Ship journeys from the north, steered and ruled over by Loki. Some versions render this 'east', and indeed, Hrym (strophe 50) and Angrboda

101

(strophe 40) are reckoned to the east. There is a 'north-facing door' in strophe 38, and pillars that stand 'before the north' in strophe 37, which suggest positions in the south; and in strophe 36 there is an 'isolated eastern mountain'. Because this verse commentary is more concerned with the energy patterns behind the symbols - rather then exact bearings - an examination of these orientations will be viewed intuitively.

East and south suggest awareness and outcome, which is where the Jotuns appear to be coming from - to bring about the final battle; whereas Loki from the north (origins) would imply retribution from 'past' deeds, or those events that have occurred prior to this moment, which becomes clear in the next line.

Coming with surety are Hella's great host of men .. to establish her laws. Death, the law of Hella's realm, is the source of life - from the physical to the spiritual. (1) Each age must come to an end, for out of darkness comes clarity. This decomposition, a process of composition-composting, must take place to assure renewal and subsequent abundance. Finally, the strophe reads Hella's 'great host' not 'Hella's Way', this latter seemingly indicating a specific direction.

..and to these, that brother Bee-Sock, in company to attack. Býleist is sometimes given as Býleipt; the former is 'bee-sock', the latter 'bee-lightening'. In all cases bees are symbolic of the soul, whereas socks are considered dirty and lowly, so this could be 'Brother Lowly Soul'. If the ending where 'leipt' this would translate as 'lightning soul', in this example, 'lowly-souls' seems more appropriate.

Reference
(1) Hella's realm. Some translations offer "Muspel".

~ ~ ~

Vol.52: *Surt journeys from the south with the sun-shining sword to overcome with craft the Gods of the Slain. [By his side] the savage and bloodthirsty tumble down like stone and rock. Treading unrestrained from Hella's Way, the Open Air - that which is clear and manifest - is split open.*

Surt journeys from the south. From the previous strophe, this direction indicates 'outcome'.

..with the sun-shining sword. This is Frey's sword.

Treading unrestrained from Hella's Way, the Open Air - that which is clear and manifest - is split open. Himinn, commonly translated as 'heaven' makes sense here as 'open air' and 'clear and manifest', for indeed, 'heaven' carries the energy of a higher or more sublime realm then that of 'sky'.

~ ~ ~

Vol.53: *Then comes forward another grief to the Protectress: that Odin moves forward against the wolf. Against Surt comes the Illustrious Bellower, [only] to die; then is removed, fallen away, Frigg's sweet essence.*

Then comes forward another grief to the Protectress. Hlin is a Goddess of Protection, companion to Frigg and seemingly here, she has been charged to protect Odin. After Baldr's death this could be the second time she was unable to successfully guard-defend one of her charges - a sore outcome for any warrior. Exclusively, this would indicate that women did take-up arms during Ragnarök.

Against Surt comes the Illustrious Bellower, [only] to die; then is removed, fallen away, Frigg's sweet essence. Beli, the Illustrious Bellower, is another name for Frey; this 'roar'-ing name, though acquired, is symbolic of his animal-Forest Lord energy. Finally, at the death of first Baldr, then Odin, and Frey - Frigg's life essence is depleted, and so, like Nanna at Baldr's death, she dies.

Some translators find in this strophe a connection between Frigg and Jord, that they are one and the same; or that Jord is mother to Frey and Freyja, wife to Njörð. This seiðr scholar has determined otherwise, or that Frigg is her own energy pattern, one far removed and as equally distinct as Jord.

Jord's name means "earth" and Frigg's name is said to mean 'one who loves'. The connection between the two comes from Snorri's translation which relates Frigg as *Fjorgyns mær*, or "Fjorgyn's maiden". According to *Lokasenna* 26, Loki says of Frigg, "you are Earth's maid", the word 'earth' here being *Fjorgyn*, and is said to be another name for Odin. In that Frigg's Hall is Fensalir or 'Marsh-Bog Hall', this does suggest an earth, albeit watery-earth connection. However, this seiðr scholar is not convinced Frigg - Goddess of the Vernal Pools - was wed to Odin alone.

In an interesting tale, Frigg is said to have wed Vili and Ve when 'Odin' had not returned after an extended period of time. Generally, when Vili and Ve are mentioned they are joined by 'Odin'; however, energy-wise this is more accurately Óð. Of note in this tale is that Óð-Odin was a ruler and when he did not return Frigg wed his brothers, which allowed them to become rulers. This would seem then that kingship is through, in this circumstance, Frigg herself (and as already pointed out, possibly a Wanic practice).

If Frigg is 'love' then this concept could easily be wed to Óð's 'divine inspiration'; and in his absence to his brothers, Vili-mind and Ve-body. Conversely, Frigg's name is rendered Fria, which implies 'delivery; free oneself'. Speculatively and loosely, Frigg co-joined with Óð-Vili-Ve could mean 'freedom of bodymind-soul', or to 'free oneself of bodymind-soul'. If she shares Hlidskjalf with Odin - able to look out upon the multiverse - then she has the ability to achieve the condition of seiðr, which is the puncturing of consciousness to look out upon the multiverse, to enter the stream of Wyrd's Well.

Already noted is Frigg's association with marshes and bogs through the name of her hall, which could link her to decomposition-dormancy-renewed life (reference strophe 39). An idea supported further by her participation in the Wild Hunt; and finally, as mother of Baldr and Hod - spiritual vision and spiritual blindness, so to speak - her energy could be that of birth and death combined.

Other clues to Frigg's energy-identity are found in the company she keeps. Her companions are: Eir, Goddess of Healing; Hlin, Goddess of Protection; Gna, Goddess of Messengers (Valkyries perhaps?), and Fulla, Goddess of Fertility.

In Scandinavia today she is seen as Orion's Belt, or Friggerock, meaning 'Frigg's Distaff'. This constellation is commonly known as the Hunter (which could be a thread back to the Wild Hunt); according to Greek myth, Orion stands next to a river with his two hunting dogs (Canis Major and Minor). Popular the world over, this series of stars is often associated with: the number three (symbolically: spiritual synthesis), a sword (perhaps in this case a distaff; symbol of time, beginnings and continuity), and 'the light of heaven' (symbol of hope).

In possible relation to strophe 50, the Greek myth further relates how Orion never shares the sky with Scorpio (the scorpion), in that the two are rivals. Certainly, when Nail Ship is set free (sign of Scorpio rising), Frigg's energy fades away (Orion sinking beneath the horizon).

In all, there appears far more to Frigg than her commonly accepted image as 'ruler of house and home', 'patroness to married women', 'goddess of childbirth and protector of children', and 'goddess of spinning, sewing, and cooking'.

~ ~ ~

Vol.54: *Expanding in greatness, son of War Father, Víðar the Wide Expansive One, moves forward against the Carrion Beast. Screaming might, full of churning, time comes to take a stand with sword towards heart! Then, his inheritance earned: father avenged!*

Expanding in greatness .. Víðar the Wide Expansive One. For all the dark imagery conjured by the wolf, Víðar is the slayer of this. His appellation, as most in this work, is both literal and symbolic. In this case Víðar's energy is that of permeation, which expresses all-knowing wisdom. As in strophe 52 where 'heaven' is rendered Open Air, the Wide Expansive One expresses sky, atmosphere, and earth - Aboveworld, Midworld, and Underworld; or perhaps the Celtic idea of land, sea, and sky. Such strength would indicate a supreme being, not in the Christian sense but in a Teutonic one, meaning a human being with divine powers. More so then Baldr then, Víðar has an aura of ascension about him.

As the godhead, or imbued with divine nature, Víðar is the indwelling un-seen and all-pervading inspiration of truth-consciousness. It is Víðar's essence then that ripens and manifests as a seed-source of the next age of existence, the worlds after Ragnarök; as such at the least he would be the god of the newly established tribes.

Screaming might, full of churning, time comes to take a stand with sword towards heart! As with Aurgelmir, Víðar's scream is primal sound, specifically here, a weapon of destruction. With this primal scream - which must hail from a psychic center within form - Víðar ends once and for all the conflicting wolf energy, that razor's balance between savage and benign, the eternal struggle of humanity with dark evil. Screaming might and hvedrung - or that which is 'full of churning' - is a solar wheel of fierce intensity, the only weapon capable of destroying the all-devouring gluttony of rapacious cruelty. This weapon, a whirling disk (perhaps a swastika), exemplifies virtue and valor over all foul and loathsome things, or Víðar's divine wisdom piercing the heart of ignorance.

Then, his inheritance earned: father avenged! The wording is specific here: avenge, as opposed to revenge. For seiðus this point is of ethical significance. Revenge stresses the idea of retaliation or implied hatred as its motivation, even self-gratification, as opposed to avenging with justice and virtue, of righting a wrong. Intent is paramount here for both seiðus and Víðar. For the former - understanding the undercurrent of both - neither word nor deed should be with malice, and for the latter, this is an act of righteous rectitude.

~ ~ ~

Vol.55-56: *Arriving next, the noble son of Hlodyn; [two missing strophes] able to walk, Odin's son meets the snake. [With great wrath] the Warder of Midgarth strikes, [causing] all men to flee their homes. Able to step nine times, Earth's son is overcome by the snake; waning, he fears not degeneration or the yoke of dominion.*

These two strophes are confused so a great deal of conjecture has been written about them.

Arriving next, the noble son of Hlodyn. Her name translates as "Earth", but is also said to be "kind friend", "little dog", "Jordar Burr" (suggesting 'Mother Earth'), and Jörd. Her name is found in north and western Germany and Friesland, where are found five inscriptions that mention her. She is said to be the mother of either-both Thor and Víðar.

Ancestral parents are often associated with either an animal form or a primal concept like 'earth' or 'sea' or 'sky'; it seems Hlodyn has both. As 'the' earth she is the place of manifestation, the realm where fire, air, and water are most apparent, or the best realm of manifestation for these elements. As a 'little dog' she would equivocate to a 'kind friend' by way of association, but it is her Germanic name that carries the most significance for seiðfolk.

Hludana, or 'Hel'-dana, is an Underworld river in Germanic folklore, and as most goddesses of this nature, are often depicted with dogs. Perhaps her sister is Nehalenia, who is also depicted with a wolf-dog, and specifically was called upon by sailors for protection at sea. Interestingly, Nehalenia is neither Celtic nor Germanic but Indo-European, which indicates she is old and well known. At the least, there are over 60 votive altars dedicated to her, prior to 100 BCE, and after that, her honor continued until the third century Common Era.

Exclusively, Hludana and Nehalenia are two of the Matrones, their energy patterns being akin to earth, sea, and sky. In this verse commentary, one combination of the Three Mothers could be: Nerthus-Erce, Jörd-Fjorgynn, and Hlodynn-Hludana.

[With great wrath] the Warder of Midgarth strikes, [causing] all men to flee their homes. Seemingly, the impact of Thor clashing with the Great Serpent causes the earth to shake, sending humans fleeing from their homes (as in an earthquake).

Able to step nine times, Earth's son is overcome by the snake. Walking is one thing, stepping with a specific reference to a number of paces is quite the other. Taking steps signifies movement towards ascension, graduating from one realm of existence to another. Nine is symbolic of the three worlds, or the triangle-ternary, meaning the final steps taken before moving on to the next level of experience. For knowledgeable seiðus this represents a 'growth process' or period of transition - often traumatic - that ends in either trauma-death or deeper wisdom. Similarly, Sámi shamans take nine steps up a tree to sit between the worlds. In the above, Thor - defender against chaos, Warder of Midgarth (the human form) - descends like a falling star, expressing the highest purpose of spirit impacting earth; or, that, which vanquishes doubt. Meaning, Thor's death has the ability to release us from attachment to the physical realm - the human fear of death and dying - so that the coils of time and space no longer hinder soul's expression. Certainly then, this could explain Thor's connections to seiðr. (1)

..waning, he fears not degeneration or the yoke of dominion. Thor's essence is released not through moral or spiritual decline or the domination of his ability or reputation, but through honor and integrity.

Reference
(1) Thor .. seiðr. Various references seem to thread Thor with seiðr:
- Glavendrup stone, 10th century, *Þur vigi þasi runar*, "May Thor hallow these runes";
- Korpbron stone, 10th century: *siþi Þórr*, "Thor work seiðr";

107

- Various stones: *þórr vigi*, "Thor protect".

~ ~ ~

Vol.57: *Sun turns to black, earth sinks gently into sea; Bright Wheel of Open Sky, star's course, [no longer seen]. Raging vapor and appointed fire compete on high, sending heat, [on the] verge of Open Sky.*

'Black sun', 'watery earth', 'motionless Wheel', 'fleeting fire', from 'low to high' - these are all opposites. Black sun is scorched earth that becomes fertile. Watery earth is limitless regeneration. A motionless Wheel is above all time and space. Fleeting fire is only temporary. From low to high is the route our soul must take, from Hella's Hall through Midworld to Tivar realms. Even in the ending the beginning is seen, as is seen in the next strophe.

~ ~ ~

Völuspá - Tree Renewed

Vol.58: *I see coming up another journey: earth from the ocean, ever-green. The eagle flies above, falling in ambush, upon the moor, catching fish.*

Another adventure awaits - a migration from one realm of existence to another. The earth, like a fetus in a womb, like Berkana, has gone through a transformation, being birthed a-green, fertile and growing, lush and vibrant. Eagles fly overhead hunting fish - spirit soaring (eagle) the realms between (moor, not earth or sea) ever evolving (hunting) through the physical multiverse (fish). Already the pace of life resumes where it left off.

~ ~ ~

Vol.59: *Pleased where the Ensi upon the Whirling-Field, to search both earth and tree, perceiving the complete victory; to remember the place of powerful and great events, and on mighty gods of ancient and hidden lore.*

To search 'both earth and tree' is to look both inward and outward, or from personal surroundings to inner-self.

~ ~ ~

Vol.60: *There shall be found in the grass, wondrous golden game-pieces, those that were the family chieftains in days of yore.*

Gold is symbolic of all things superior, the game and its pieces displaying an effort to contain or control the potent forces of nature. Such a devise reflects their spiritual determination; however, it is more rational than spiritual in that games are exterior means of creating certainty and continuity.

~ ~ ~

Vol.61: *Then shall unsown fields wax, producing plenty, misfortune a memory far away; all has improved and as remembered, Baldr comes. Hod the Warrior and Baldr will make ready Hropt's home for the Gods of Victory; well-grown and understanding [are now] those Gods of the Slain. I am skilled in such visions, yet still you seek more?*

Fields that produce abundantly are symbolic of limitless possibility. In this world transformed there are no concerns, and as 'remembered' or has happened before, Baldr returns, and exclusively, Hod returns full-sighted. Generally, entities with one eye speak only half-truths, while blindness denotes obscured truth; here Hod stands equal to Baldr in the full truth of full-vision.

..well-grown and understanding [are now] those Gods of the Slain. The suggestion here is that the divine powers have been refined, made stronger and better for their ordeal.

None will survive the intense burning except those of iron will. Only those who stand determined against persecution and isolation in a dreary and indifferent world will be transformed by the flames of Surt into souls of golden light, of golden will. Odin and Freyja intend for these 'chosen ones' to be their warriors, hand-picked for this task alone. Whoever they may be they will make good for all human souls against time and for the sake of eternal Truth. Those that fight in the great multiversal struggle against the forces of disintegration do not fight in vain, but victoriously alongside the forces of life, the bright wights, the great Tivar.

Baldr will lead a great host through flames of the Great End; he will arrive unscathed to see the Golden Age. Great fighters of blood and Faith - whose deserving of honor and minni-rites - shall re-seed the green forests and blue seas, building horgrs upon inviolate mountain peaks, leaders of Midworld reborn.

Vili is there, and Víðar and Váli (sons of Odin), and Modi and Magni (sons of Thor), Baldr and Hod, all reborn. Lif and Lifthrasir will survive hidden within World Tree, grandsires to Midworld renewed. These hands make Midworld green and fertile again.

Alfrodul, Sunna's daughter, arrives in her radiant wagon; a new sun rises. And Gimle, the great and golden hall where all shall live, will be a place of safety and plenty - with Brimir as its beating heart (one of Gimle's Halls).

Thor's sons could be the new Waggoner's of Open Sky, in a vehicle drawn by Tanngrisnir and Tanngnjostr. These goats represent maternal implications, superiority and high peaks. Symbolically, they are Capricorn - with a goat's body and fish's tail – representing the involutive and evolutive possibilities, or the return to and departure from the wheel of rebirth.

Frey and Surt are the inside and outside of Ginnunga-gap's bowl, manifesting all potential found therein. Frey is the essence of Sunna, which is vibrant life; Surt has the essence of Lightening, which is annihilation. Frey is the faithful and original pattern of creation, the return to a Golden Age, Surt the fierce wind of destruction, and Ginnunga-gap the fathomless blessing, the timeless serenity, the soothing stillness.

~ ~ ~

Vol.62: *Then can Hoenir choose the blood-rods; and the brother's sons, first-cousins, will colonize twofold, Windhome far and wide. I am skilled in such visions, yet still you seek more?*

Hoenir is an aspect of mind, credited with gifting Ask and Embla with 'sense'. Later he is sent with Mimir as a hostage to the Wana; in this his role as conscious mind is more clearly seen to Mimir's subconscious or deep mind of the Well. Exclusively, Hoenir is a sacrificial priest whose actions signify that by the flowing of blood danger has past. Taking up the blood-rods assures a continued relationship between the realms above and below.

..the brother's sons, first-cousins, will colonize twofold, Windhome far and wide. These two are, energy-wise, the son's of Hod and Baldr; combined they will oversee Windhome, or the entirety of Open Sky (heaven). These sons become the guardians of breath-life, of fertilizing breeze and towering storm, of speech and communication and the manifestation of all new things.

It has been noted in other translations-interpretations that these last strophes do not mention women; clearly the presence of sons speaks otherwise (also implied in strophe 53).

~ ~ ~

Vol.63: *I see a standing homestead, embellished and beautiful like the sun; golden roof upon Gimlé [of the] Cut-Stone. There shall the worthy folk dwell with endless delight, benefiting greatly.*

111

This home of cut-stone and golden roof stands in Windhome, or Open Sky-heaven, so it exists in the realm above. Some have translated Gimlé as 'fire-shelter', its energy and appearance however is closer to cut gemstones.

~ ~ ~

This next strophe is generally regarded as a Christian insertion, something this seiðr scholar agrees with; therefore it is irrelevant to the nature of this commentary.

~ ~ ~

Vol.64: *Comes yet the [staff] flying dark dragon, gleaming snake undulating down Dark Mountain; bedecked with feathers - flying steady above - Nidhogg, Downward-Smashing and near. Now my memory sinks, [ebbing] down.*

Some have seen in this last strophe a futile future where Nidhogg persists in haunting humanity. Intuitively, there appears to be a runic code in the second line of this strophe.

Kømr inn dimmi / dreki fliúgandi,
naðr fránn, neðan / frá Niðafiöllom;
bersk í fiöðrom - flýgr völl yfir -
Niðhöggr, nái / nú mun sökkvask.

Which could be viewed as: naðr-Nauthiz, fránn-Fehu, neðan-Nauthiz, frá-Fehu, Niðafiöllom-Nauthiz/Fehu, loosely meaning: necessity and creative energy, each repeated three times. (1)

Nauthiz can be threaded to both Surt and Skuld, signifying 'necessity' and the need to 'attend to a problem'. This rune rules Nifelheim, where Nidhogg resides. (2) Additionally, nauthiz is cohesion, self-preservation and recognition, comprehension and supreme joy. (3) Fehu is 'movable wealth', something that should be 'given away freely', and personal 'reputation'. (2) Additionally, fehu is the Folksoul in relation to self, perception and utilization of sacred space, unification of will, and harmony in all the worlds. (3)

This seiðr scholar has utilized the refrain as a kvæði, "chant", and in so doing has discerned the 'gleaming snake' as the integrated bodymind-soul, as pure energy and consciousness, an activator of psychic probability; and the 'dark mountain' or 'moonless mountain' as a realm without measure.

(4)   The moon, from Indo-European lore, indicates the great cosmic dragon, so here - in this 'dark' or moonless place - is found Nidhogg as Wyrd itself. In short, the trance induced by this kvæði has lead to a realm of immortality, or the highest principle of consciousness-illumination; this then is a profound opportunity: to place soul in the vast stream of Wyrd. A more fitting end for the Folksoul cannot be imagined.

References

(1) Runic code. A coined phrase by this seiðr scholar to denote a possible hidden meaning in Lore strophes or stanzas.   Another such possible example is *Havamal* 144, which advises the would-be rune crafter to: 'write and read', 'paint and prove', 'ask and offer', 'send and spend'. In Old Norse, these words are: rista and ráða, fá and freista, bíða and blóta, senda and sóa, respectively.   This would render the strophe as: R.F.B.S., or Raido, Fehu, Berkana, and Sowulo. Runically, aside from being used as a galdr, the meaning here can be: journey and initiation, fee and wealth, birth and sacred journey, highest will and intent, respectively.   And like *Völuspá* 64, this seiðr scholar has utilized the refrain as a kvæði to discern: the yielding of information (Raido) within spacious reality (Fehu) so observation can turn inwards, establishing the foothold of inner being (Berkana) to express the power of divine word through right speech (Sowulo). Assuredly this is runic Rita, or the true value of runes.

(2) Nauthiz and fehu freely related from *Northern Mysteries and Magick*; by F. Aswynn; 1990.

(3) Nauthiz and fehu from the author's interpretation.

(4) Kvæði, "chant". As an endnote (no pun intended), and already referenced, Bergelmir is the endnote of the world and so survives Ragnarök as the substance of all renewed forms, the new keynote of creation.

~ ~ ~

Conclusion - Seiðr as Wyrd Consciousness

Seiðr, as Wyrd consciousness, is a non-event that explains the difficulty encountered in defining and therefore understanding its primal state of existence. However, once consciousness has been penetrated there is an accompanying realization that one has access to vast reservoirs of ineffable knowledge and wisdom. Far from being a new realm of spiritual inquiry this process of knowingness - or profound perception and all-encompassing awareness - is intuition beyond intuition. Meaning, seiðr is re-cognition.

Völuspá allows a glimpse into the current of consciousness, a means to understand the tumultuous sea of seiðr and its unfathomed depths of realization. Which is why seiðr is no idling curiosity or intellectual pursuit but an exploration of transpersonal reality that results in a profound inner urge to reveal the secrets of life. Once peered upon - past illusionary personal reflection - this Well compels those who seek its depths to share their transformation through service to the Folksoul.

Seiðr is a condition of connectedness, the philosophy of inner nature, and the Folksoul's heart - which is the spiritual nature of those who originated and carry Heathenry's distinctive culture and traditional way of life and living. Consciousness' parabolic orbit can only be accessed through seiðr, which causes the whirlpool of internal knowing to bubble and seethe, attracting the descent of Ginnunga-gapic energy.

After this verse commentary what remains is:
- "What prompts this powerful form of consciousness extension, connection, and relatedness?"
- "How, precisely does the condition of seiðr come about?" and,
- "To what extent does mythic-consciousness become a part of individual-everyday being?"

Because seiðr is the one device that unites all forms of soulcrafting - from spá to galdr to runes to healing to wortcunning - it is the most fundamental shift of perception that radically restructures experiential awakening and the one activity that creates a new and liberating gestalt of wholeness. Its study is paramount to success in every spiritual endeavor.

Völuspá - Prophecy of the Völva

Introduction to Heid

Vol.28 and 29: *Alone I sat outside when the aged one arrived, the wise Ensi, and looked me in the eye. I challenged him, "What do you ask me? Why do you try me? I know [and grant] everything Odin; like, where you hid your eye, in Mimir's Well. Mimir drinks mead every morning from your pledge. Yet, do you understand?"*

Vol.27: *I know all your secrets Odin. I know where Heimdallr's hearing (ear) is hidden, under the sky-reaching sacred tree. There I see a stream overflowing with muddy waters - from your pledge! Do you understand yet? Do you?*

Vol.30. *Striding to my harrow, he furnished me with rings, so the wise-sayings [the sound advice] could be prophecised from my staff; for my consciousness knows consciousness, the existence of everything.*

Vol.1: *Silence then I asked of the hallowed kindred, and from Heimdallr's children, both high and low born. Agreeable to you War-father, I shall speak of well before the counted time, relating ancient tales, put forth to promote and further all men.*

Before the Beginning

[Interpolation] Ginnunga-gap was there, beginning before beginning, seething and churning void of nothingness from which first things merge. Blessed skull and cauldron, radii of zenith and nadir, keeper of three Wells and three roots, soul of all seeds, it is the all of nothing, the nothing of all.

Vol.3: *First, in ancient time, was old Aurgelmir's fixed abode,[the triple enclosure] when there was no sand or sea, no cooling wave. There was no earth anywhere, no heaven above, only Ginnunga-gap, the seething void, and nowhere herb.*

Vol.2: *I remember well the household of giants, when they fed me food with nobility. Nine residing worlds I know - nine far-reaching - World Tree to praise and decorate, before the earth was new.*

Vol.5: *Sunna, companion to Mani, came from the south; [she] cast her right hand over heaven's rim, not knowing yet in which quarter her homestead should be. Stars were not certain, having no knowledge where they [should] steer and guide, [not knowing] which place their quarter should be. Mani was not certain, what strength his quarter should be.*

Vol.4: *Buri's grandsons [then] raised-up the flatland to be seen, fashioning the praiseworthy [and glorious] Midworld. Sun shone from the south, warming the hearthstones, and the ground became overgrown with green garden leeks [[garlic]].*

The Order of Things

Vol.6: *Then went the ruling powers, [the decision makers], to their tranquil and proud stools of decision-making; the holy gods gathering in council. To Night and New Moon they gave names, Morning they named, and Mid-day as well; and Afternoon, and Evening, for the first and next years - [their ancient beginnings] - to be counted, [to trace their descent].*

[Interpolation and Vol.7] *Churning Well's whirlpool below, heaven's whirlpool above, Grotti is walked by nine maidens. World above, the Ensi met on the Whirling-Field, building stone altars in high places. They laid hearths, forged riches, wrought tongs and tools.*

Vol.8: *They played at tables, glad and cheerful were they, and there was no lack of gold. Until three giants came from Jotunheim on matters relating to marriage, very loathsome they were to the Ensi.*

Vol.17: *Then came three together - of the rare host - powerful and loved Ensi out of their enclosure. They found on land, light of availing might, Ask and Embla, loose of the thread of life.*

Vol.18: *They had no inhaling breath, no soul, nor had they inherited a noble mind, no blood or warm voice, no good color or moral. Inhaling Breath gave Óð, Noble Mind gave Hoenir, Blood and Warm Voice gave Lodur, and good hue.*

Vol.19: *I know a Yew that stands, Yggdrasil it is called; a high tree sprinkled with white clay, and there comes the dew - marking the tree - falling from the open river valley. It stands evergreen above Urd's Well.*

Vol.20: *From there came maidens - being friendly and knowing much magic - three from the sea, which is below the tree. Become one is called, another Becoming - they advise from staves - and Shall-be is third. Wise laws they had, of life they murmured from cuttings of wood. Swelling is the tree's bark, the strands of fate for men.*

The Great War

Vol.21: *I remember the folk-battle, the first in the realm, where Gold-draught they supported on an anvil's point, yoking her in the High Hall, with their hands burning her. Three times burned - three times! - three times born again, still she lives on.*

Vol.22: *Heid she is called when she arrives at built houses, choosing well to seethe, to foretell, all sense-consciousness - marking and riding her staff. To chant with knowing, to bring ease and comfort through mindful enchanting; ever washing the head with sweet and fragrant odor, there to rid ill-brewings.*

Vol.23: *Then went the ruling powers [the decision makers] to their tranquil and proud stools [the seats of decision-making]; the holy gods gathering in council. Whether the Ensi are bound-obliged to pay tribute, or are the gods bound-obliged to share brotherhood?*

Vol.24: *Odin hurled [a spear] over a corner of heaven, over the folk - that was the folk-battle, first ever where they lived. Broken then were the wooden walls, the boards of Ensigart; with prowess the Wana made themselves unharmed by spear, fighting unharmed, treading on [Ensi] ground.*

[Interpolated] *Upon the Great Ones came the responsibility for frith; kinship to assure accord in all worlds. The blessing songs of Grotti rang loud and pure with pleasing sound. Into this air did the Great Ones - Jotun, Ensi, and Wana alike - exchange hostages.*

Continued Conflict

[Interpolated] *Then came blowing wind, hissing like a serpent, Blast offering to rebuild the great Ensigart walls. From Midnight Sun to Burning Wheel did he toil with proud steed Svadilfari, seeking sun and moon and Freyja as payment. Trickery his only reward, bloodshed on Ensigart's ground.*

Vol.25: *Then went the ruling powers [the decision makers] to their tranquil and proud stools [the seats of decision-making]; the holy gods gathering in council. Who lifted into the air a crafty mix of discord, whether to release to the Jotun's quarter [their direction, area] the divine inheritance, the maiden of good conduct.*

Vol.26: *Thor alone was troubled then, stifling his wrath, he seldom sits still when hearing such things. Violated and dead are the oaths, words sworn to - speech having lost its strength, the middle ground torn asunder.*

Vol.27 [Interpolated]: *On Midworld this is why you sent the World Brightener Odin, why you sent the white Wanic fire, the bringer of nine virtues. Blessed Father Heimdallr, the fire-auger, teacher of the human soul, son of nine mothers; he alone could do what you - Warlord - could not. Reconciliation you sought and treaty too Odin, but no friend to accord have you ever been.*

Baldr's Wyrd

Vol.31. *While on High I saw the Valkyries, through my consciousness, arriving from afar. Clearly I remember their horses' weaving ride to the Godfolk. Skuld - duty bound to collect the debt, knowing how to discern knowledge - assuring all have their due, and Bone-Skinner busy at work behind her; [with them are] God-daughter, Battle, Running-Concealment, and Gory-Skinned-Joint. Now has their place been numbered among the Father's Host, set to perform their sacrifice are the Choosers of the Slain, upon the green grassy plain.*

Vol.32: *I see Baldr, blood-smeared god, Odin's child, thread of life fading away. A great beam had grown up, well-shapen, and with a round stick, hoary with age, was laid flat on the ground; greatly praised and decorated, the fair and beautiful mistletoe.*

Vol.33: *Alone had this plant to answer for the maiming, though greatly praised and decorated, being seen by all - vexed and baneful shaft - bringing risk and danger. Hod shot from a bow at his brother Baldr; Odin's son Váli born quickly, at one night old fighting [his brother's killer].*

Vol.34: *Nevertheless, he never took a hand to comb his hair - being the brave warrior he would never be free or at ease unless he fulfilled his task first; he was already aflame for a fight and ready to build a funeral pyre against Baldr's adversary. And Frigg did frown and decry this act at her Marshy Homestead, great danger now to the Slain's Hall! I go farther inward speaking, what more sensibility do you need?*

Forces Gather

Vol.35: *From here I see the Wailing Vali, slaughtered, fighting, daring more against the hostility; strong he is against the troop who dares assault him. Bound and chained with fetters I saw, under Grotti, the Turning Wheel, lying there with proud temper was Loki, anchored in disgrace. There sits Victorious Delight, Sigyn, not able to revenge one against many; protecting her husband with her goodness, her duty and homage to him. I have demonstrated my consciousness to be existent and deep, to what end do you seek?*

Vol.36: *It is not then unmet that from an isolated eastern mountain, surrounded by a venomous dale of daggers and swords, came Fierce- and Cruel-Sheath.*

Vol.37: *Pillars stood before the north, marking the Dark Moon Fields (where are found the mounds of völva's). Departed souls come out of there rich with gold from Sindar's family, him of the Sparking Iron-Scales. Deeper within are pillars of un-cold, where is found Jotun's beer hall, Dashing of Surf is called.*

Vol.38: *I saw a homestead standing far from the sun; on the Woven Rope of Corpses there is a north-facing doorway. Poison falls in drops from a contentious opening, a private room above which is strong with snakes, very distressful, a sly and crooked place.*

Vol.39: *I saw then, wading in a burdened stream, perjured men and murderous outlaws, and those who otherwise confuse the ear of a woman with false-intimacy. In this place, the Dark Biter, Nidhogg, defiles the forward wave of newly departed souls, and a strangler deceives existence. Inwardly I know these things, would you know more and what?*

Dark Scheming

Vol.40: *Eastwards sits an Old One in the Iron Forest - there feeding Fenris' kind; and it happens that one is fit above any other - the Lunar Year Destroyer - in troll shape.*

Vol.41: *Filled with death's struggle he comes, beyond rescue he wishes for death; rust-colored, seeking only evil, his home is an iron bog oozing with blood. And it comes to pass that the sun is wounded, its shine becomes withered and summer cannot be found; ill-natured is the wind from that quarter. I am skilled! What more would you know!*

Vol.42: *Sitting there on the burial cairn, playing a harp with sly cunning, sits gleaming and golden Eggther the Useful Egg, bodyguard and caretaker to the Gýgjar. The fine and light-red gallows cock crows from the goose-wood, Fjalarr he is called.*

Vol.43: *Crows Golden-Comb over the gods, rousing from sleep those free-born who dwell with the Father of Hosts. Yet before that, the other roars from beneath earth, a loathsome and destructive cock in Hella's Hall.*

Vol.44: *Now with building violence Garm stands before the great door of Highest Cave - remembering when the rope broke and the wolf ran free. I have great learning - powerful charms to assist me - for further still I see guilt fall: God's Doom! So to battle, you Gods of Victory!*

World's Doom

Vol.45: *Brothers will beat and bring death to each other, cousins will be spoiled by adultery; there is difficulty in the world and great whoredom. Shield Age, Axe Age: shields - discernment and knowledge are trapped and torn asunder. Wind Age, Wolf Age: already the world is degraded and overthrown. No memory will remain of man being reverent, of showing respect, to another.*

Vol.46-47: *Plays Mim at denial, but the measure of doom is against this guiling kin - soon struck down by Screaming Horn - for it happens that Heimdallr's horn of defense is held aloft. Shaken by the sound, Yggdrasil's Ash stands, the Tree of Life groaning; Odin speaks to Mim's greatness, and the Jotun is set free. Come the dreadful on Hella's Road, Surt leading the way, those of like-mind swallowing all before them.*

Vol.48: *Consider the Gods, consider the Alfar - all of Jotunheim is clashing! The gods have assembled, dwarves - sprouting from steep rock - groan at the stone door. Should I reveal more or what?*

Vol.49: *Now, with great mastery does Garm stand before the Highest Cave. The fastener is removed - torn asunder - greed runs free. Much have I helped you, teaching what I know, further still comes God's Doom - to battle, you Gods of Victory!*

Vol.50: *Old Age Sickness comes from the east with linden-tree raised high. Waves are beaten by serpent turning, the Vast-Great Monster churns Jotun-wrath; then, eagles screaming tears asunder pale waning moon. Nail Ship is set free!*

Vol.51: *Ship journeys from the north, steered and ruled over by Loki. Coming with surety are Hella's great host of men - with very severe monsters - to establish her laws; and to these, that brother Bee-Sock, in company to attack.*

Vol.52: *Surt journeys from the south with the sun-shining sword to overcome with craft the Gods of the Slain. [By his side] the savage and bloodthirsty tumble down like stone and rock. Treading unrestrained from Hella's Way, the Open Air - that which is clear and manifest - is split open.*

Vol.53: *Then comes forward another grief to the Protectress: that Odin moves forward against the wolf. Against Surt comes the Illustrious Bellower, [only] to die; then is removed, fallen away, Frigg's sweet essence.*

Vol.54: *Expanding in greatness, son of War Father, Víðar the Wide Expansive One, moves forward against the Carrion Beast. Screaming might, full of churning, time comes to take a stand with sword towards heart! Then, his inheritance earned: father avenged!*

Vol.55-56: *Arriving next, the noble son of Hlodyn; [two missing strophes] able to walk, Odin's son meets the snake. [With great wrath] the Warder of Midgarth strikes, [causing] all men to flee their homes. Able to step nine times, Earth's son is overcome by the snake; waning, he fears not degeneration or the yoke of dominion.*

Vol.57: *Sun turns to black, earth sinks gently into sea; Bright Wheel of Open Sky, star's course, [no longer seen]. Raging vapor and appointed fire compete on high, sending heat, [on the] verge of Open Sky.*

Tree Renewed

Vol.58: *I see coming up another journey: earth from the ocean, ever-green. The eagle flies above, falling in ambush, upon the moor, catching fish.*

Vol.59: *Pleased where the Ensi upon the Whirling-Field, to search both earth and tree, perceiving the complete victory; to remember the place of powerful and great events, and on mighty gods of ancient and hidden lore.*

Vol.60: *There shall be found in the grass, wondrous golden game-pieces, those that were the family chieftains in days of yore.*

Vol.61: *Then shall unsown fields wax, producing plenty, misfortune a memory far away; all has improved and as remembered, Baldr comes. Hod the Warrior and Baldr will make ready Hropt's home for the Gods of Victory; well-grown and understanding [are now] those Gods of the Slain. I am skilled in such visions, yet still you seek more?*

Vol.62: *Then can Hoenir choose the blood-rods; and the brother's sons, first-cousins, will colonize, twofold, Windhome far and wide. I am skilled in such visions, yet still you seek more?*

Vol.63: *I see a standing homestead, embellished and beautiful like the sun; golden roof upon Gimlé [of the] Cut-Stone. There shall the worthy folk dwell with endless delight, benefiting greatly.*

Vol.64: *Comes yet the [staff] flying dark dragon, gleaming snake undulating down Dark Mountain; bedecked with feathers - flying steady above - Nidhogg, Downward-Smashing and near. Now my memory sinks, [ebbing] down.*

Glossary

Alfar: Elves, and sometimes Disir. Specific to this verse commentary the Alfar are 'star entities'.

Alu: Literally, "ale"; a mystic drink. Implied Luck and mystic might, or mægen.

Blot and Faining: Both are sacred rites - the former includes blood the latter does not.

Dis or Disir: Female ancestors, minor goddesses, and Valkyries.

Ensi and Wana: The Germanic names for the Aesir and Vanir.

Folksoul: Specific to this verse commentary, Folksoul is the spiritual nature of those who originated and carry Heathenry's distinctive culture and traditional way of life and living.

Galdr: One of the Soulcrafts. Galdr is mystic incantation, similar to mantra perhaps.

Ginnunga-gap: The Great Seething Void of All and Nothing.

Gýgjar: Female Jotuns (giants).

Heið: Gullveig reborn. Literally, "bright, clear".

Horgr: A stone alter, or alter made from stones piled one upon the other.

Lore: A collective word for Northern European, pre-Christian mythology, folk traditions, and historical accounts.

Mægen: Literally, "might, strength"; implied 'mystic might'. Specific to this verse commentary, lifeforce, or prana / chi. Mægen is the prime moving force within everything perceived by the senses, both inner and outer, but also independent of the realm of appearance.

Midworld: Earth. Often in conjunction with Above- and Underworld, or realms above and below.

Minni: Memory, to remember well, the mind of remembrance.

Óð: Literally, "divine inspiration"; also, the soul residing within humans.

Óð, Vili, and Ve: The reflections of being, or 'soul', 'sense', and 'motion-hue'; sometimes referred to as soul, mind, and body, respectively.

Ragnarök: The doom or destruction of the gods.

Rita: Primordial, Natural and Organic Law; Ginnunga-gapic Law.

Samal: A sacred drinking feast that shapes Wurt and Urlag (Ørlög).

Seiðr: One of the Soulcrafts. Specific to this verse commentary, seiðr is the penetration of transcendental consciousness, the condition of trance; the exploration of transpersonal reality and a science or means "to know or understand" experiential awakening.

Seiðu, Seiðus: A coined term to denote a soulcrafter who engages in trance or Wyrd consciousness.

Sippe: A kindred or family unit.

Soulcraft: Mystical or magical application of a learned skill to affect someone's soul or being.

Tide: A seasonal fluctuation, such as from spring to summer, or from vernal equinox to summer solstice.

Tivar and Vettir: Literally, "Gods" and 'wights; Alfar'.

Spá: One of the soulcrafts. In particular, 'far-seeing' or 'second sight'.

Thau and Troth: Customs or virtues.

Þular: A wise seer and individual who guides the Thau-Troth of a Sippe or Tribe.

Trú: Faith and honor.

Urlag and Ørlög: Literally, "primal layers". Urlag is the primal layers of experience or every experience laid one atop the other; it is all past action that influences present reality.

Varðlokkur, Vardlokkur: 'Warder's song; warding charm; ward-allure, ward-entice'. A mystic song that induces trance and/or attracts attendant spirits or guardians to a soulcrafter.

Völva: A wise woman and practitioner of one or more soulcrafts, possible to include seiðr.

Völuspá: Literally, "Prophecy of the Völva

Wort cunning: Knowledge of and skill with herbs; literally, 'herb knowledge; herb wisdom'.

Wyrd: Also known as Wurt. Wurt is working *in* and through cause and affect; namely, 'past', 'present', and 'future'.

Book Hoard

Primary Sources of Translation

Diederichs, E. *Thule - Altnordische Dichtung und Prosa, zweiter Band*, Germany, 1934

Niedner, F. *Edda - zweiter Band / Götterdichtung und Spruchdichtung*, Germany, 1932

Zoega, G.T. *A Concise Dictionary of Old Icelandic*, London, 2000

Primary Sources of Symbology

Dallapiccola, A. *Dictionary of Hindu Lore and Legend*, London, 2002

Friberg, E. *The Kalevala: Epic of the Finnish People*, Finland, 1989

Jung, C.G. *Symbols of Transformation*, London, 1956

Lakoff, G., and Johnson, M. *Metaphors We Live By*, Chicago, 1980

Lehner, E. *Symbols, Signs and Signets*, New York, 1962

Lidstone, R.A. *Studies in Symbology*, New York, 1997

Papus (pseudonym for: Gerard Anaclet Vincent Encausse). *Elementary Treatise on Occultism*, New York, 1950

Teillard, A. *Symbology of Sound*, New York, 1951

Thomas, N.L. *Irish Symbols of 3500 BC*, Dublin, 1988

Primary Sources of Shamanism

Balzer, M. *Shamanism: Soviet Studies of Traditional Religion in Siberia and Central Asia*, New York, 1990

Kalweit, H. *Dreamtime and Inner Space - the World of the Shaman*, Boston, 1984
- *Shamans, Healers, and Medicine Men*, Boston, 1987

- *Das Totenbuch der Germanen - Die Edda, Die Wurzeln eines wilden Volkes*, 2001

References - General

Blain, J. *Nine Worlds of Seid-Magic - Ecstasy and Neo-Shamanism in North European Paganism*, London, 2002

Bord, J. and C. *Earth Rites*, London, 1982

Bray, O. The *Elder or Poetic Edda, Commonly Known As Saemund's Edda*, New York, 1982

Caesar J. *Gallic War*, London, 1917

Davidson, H.R.E. *Myths and Symbols in Pagan Europe*, New York, 1988.
- *The Lost Beliefs of Northern Europe*, London, 1993.
- *The Road to Hel*, New York, 1968

Fee, C.R., and Leeming, D.A. *Gods, Heroes, and Kings - The Battle for Mythic Britain*, New York, 2001

Gordon, E. *Introduction to Old Norse*, New York, 1981

Grimm, J. *Teutonic Mythology*, New York, 1966

Hutton, R. *The Pagan Religions of the Ancient British Isles - Their Nature and Legacy*, London, 1991

Jung, C. *Psychology of Alchemy*, Frankfurt, 1953

Lethbridge, T.C. *Gogmagog, The Buried Gods*, London, 1957

Mallory, J.P. *In Search of the Indo-Europeans*, London, 1989

Munch, P.A. *Norse Mythology - Legends of Gods and Heroes*, New York, 1942

Orchard, A. *Cassell's Dictionary of Norse Myth & Legend*, London, 1997

Rees, A. & Rees, B. *Celtic Heritage - Ancient Tradition in Ireland and Wales*, London, 1961

Rudenko, S. *Frozen Tombs of Siberia*, London, 1953

Sivananda, Swami *What Becomes of the Soul After Death*, India, 1979

Smyth, D. *A Guide to Irish Mythology*, Dublin, 1988

Summers, M. *Geography of Witchcraft*, New Jersey, 1963

Tacitus, P.C. *Agricola* and *Germania*, New York, 1971

Von Franz, M.L. *C.G. Jung, His Myth in Our Time*, 1975

Yeats W.B. *Ideas of Good and Evil,* London, 1901

References - Throughout

Numerous references are interspersed in this verse commentary, including individual Eddic tales, Immramas, Vedas, Upanishads, and independently written and/or internet articles.

Writer's Biography

Yngona Desmond was raised to value both Celtic folklore and Theosophy. For over 35 years she has lived, studied, and taught a mystical and spiritual lifestyle. Her dedication to Heathen esoterica is found, among other places, in *Thuleheim - A Knowledge Base*, a collection of occult lore from the Northern European, pre-Christian traditions, that she maintains with fellow soulcrafter Garrick Cartwright.

Desmond is a spiritual traveler and sacred pilgrim, having traversed much of Europe - from Ireland to Italy - visiting and honoring sacred sites. By actively monitoring Ley-lines, chanting to re-tune and re-align ancient stones, assisting local Guardians with energy clean-up, and reconnecting in a non-invasive manner with primal and ancestral energies, she lives intimately in the flow of those deep and mystical currents that course across our planet.

Unwaveringly, she lives in many realms simultaneously. Having never been Christian, her worldview is unique in that she brings a deeply rooted connectedness and profound sense of understanding to the seemingly impenetrable depths of Heathen mysticism and Seiðr philosophy.

Made in the USA
Middletown, DE
15 January 2022